Telling War Stories

TELLING WAR STORIES

An Infantryman's Account of Life and Death in World War II

DONALD WEINSTEIN

ISBN: 9798713795016

FOREWORD

My father was born on March 13, 1926 in Rochester, New York, and died on December 13, 2015 in Tucson, Arizona. The eight stories in this volume are almost the entirety of his autobiographical output. The first three are about his upbringing in Rochester, as the son of Jewish immigrants, and the last five are about his combat experience as an infantryman during the last few months of the Second World War. He first entered combat just inside Germany while still 18 years old, in February of 1945 right after the Battle of the Bulge. On VE day, he was in a field hospital being treated for trench foot, which had been exacerbated by how badly his standard-issue army boots had fit his size 13A feet. He was sent back to the States shortly after treatment, so no liberating of concentration camps or roaming the streets of Munich or Paris for him.

He never said much about his war experiences when I was growing up in the 1960s, even though I would have been delighted to hear more. Most of my friends' fathers were Korean War vets or otherwise had been in the Army sometime later in the 1950s. It was not until much later that I realized how relatively rare my father's experiences had been. He had done exactly what an eight-year-old boy thought a WWII "army man" did: he had walked across Germany, shooting at Nazis with the equipment he could carry on foot, sleeping in fox holes, and never bathing. He did not drive a Jeep or fly a fighter plane. He did not stop to capture any Nazi memorabilia. And when I was growing up he did not like guns or camping or volunteering. He had had a short experience as a foot soldier and he knew there was no glamour or heroism in it. He had been a G.I.—government issue—in an army made up of young civilians, having started out from all walks of life and now returning to their pre-war lives. But, first they had to make it home.

Once, when my father was probably in his sixties and fitfully working on these stories, he told me that he knew he could have written more had he started much earlier. He said that by the time he had gotten around to putting pen to paper, he just could not really remember much detail; and he feared that he risked inaccuracy were he to strain to remember more than he still saw clearly in his mind. I know he was working on at least one other story when he died, but I do not have it. It would have been interesting to hear more from him about the war's end in Bavaria, and I would have been interested in his immediate post-war experiences as well, although other readers might have found that less compelling.

There is no doubt in my mind that the war changed him. He had been a callow youth, marked by his parents' immigrant experience, destined (he thought then) to escape their workaday drudgery by becoming a doctor, a dentist, or a lawyer. Somehow, after his stint in the Army, he returned to Rochester only briefly, and soon thereafter went to the University of Chicago on the G.I. Bill, racing through his courses and earning his B.A.

in 1948 and his M.A. in 1950. He could not tell me later anything about Chicago's hipper distractions. I do not think he ever knew who Muddy Waters was, and he never went to see Leadbelly; although he did tell me he once saw Arthur Koestler speak at the U, remembering that he, Koestler, was protested by the campus Stalinists. He went on to the University of Iowa at Iowa City, where he pursued his doctorate.

By then, he was a changed man, intellectually, at least. He was not interested in money or possessions, but he had a field of study. Academically, the 1950s were good to ambitious historians. He went to Italy (and took a vacation in Germany with the visiting German Jewish refugee, George Mosse) on a Fulbright scholarship, earned his Ph.D. in 1957, and by 1960, he had a tenure track professorship at a respectable state university. He also had a wife, two small children, and a mission to stake his claim as a serious scholar in a cozy academic discipline that required long spells in Florence, Italy—a great place to be in the 1960s. He had come quite a way from his immigrant Jewish upbringing by the time I knew him. I cannot imagine how radically different his life would have been had he become a doctor, lawyer, or dentist, and stayed in Rochester in the 1950s. I will just have to credit the U.S. Army and World War II for him missing that entirely different and more conventional life. Obviously, I would not have been the person I am had he done so. Indeed, I would likely not even have been born.

Although he had been recognized in various ways and at different times by the university historians who were his peers, his obituary in The New York Times[*] may have been the closest

---

[*] https://www.nytimes.com/2015/12/31/books/donald-weinstein-influential-historian-on-the-renaissance-dies-at-89.html

he ever got to gaining recognition in the wider world. Indeed, since he respected the Times as an established and discriminating source on culture and letters, its full-page account of his life and work would have meant a lot to him.

Jonathan Weinstein
Austin, Texas
July 2019

TABLE OF CONTENTS

1.

EIN SHAINER YUNG

L ike most loves, my love for books entered through the senses. On days when the Reading Lady came to Number 8 School in Rochester, New York, she brought her stock of treasures, *A Child's Garden of Verses*, *Mother Goose Stories*, *Silver Pennies*, Grimm's and Anderson's fairy tales, among other delights. For a whole magical hour, she read to us first-graders, her tone musical, her voice gentle and controlled, unlike most of the voices I heard around me. I loved not only the stories, but the books themselves—their pictures, their smell of ink and glue, the rustle of glossy pages delicately turned under the Reading Lady's manicured hand. They say the physical part of love diminishes in time and, if the love is well-founded and constant, is compensated for by calmer pleasures of thought and feeling; but, since those days in 1932, and after a lifetime of taking in my hands manuscripts, early printed books, archival documents, and even the banal standardized products of modern printing presses, I have never lost the sensual thrill of seeing, touching and smelling the vellum, paper, cloth, leather, and ink of books.

Every day, when my sister Edith, five years older than I and a reader, returned from school, I nagged her for "just one more story." After I learned to read, she schlepped books from the public library for me. When I turned eight, Edie announced that I could now get my own books: we would go to the library together. Miraculously, she got permission from my mother (her step-mother) who was ever fearful of the dangers that awaited me, her only child, in the world beyond the limits of our Jewish neighborhood. Edie even managed to enlist her in the preparations. Such excitement! That first parentless expedition required proper clothes, shined shoes, clean handkerchief, and a packed lunch.

The nearest branch of the public library was on the opposite side of the river, almost foreign territory for our family. Getting there required a long journey by foot, down busy, previously forbidden, streets and across the mighty granite-arched Veterans' Memorial Bridge spanning the deep, still-uncolonized, gorge of the Genesee. Midway over the bridge, Edie pointed out the bronze plaque grimly informing pedestrians that two workmen had lost their lives to provide this crossing—for me the gift of passage from deprivation to enlightenment. On the other side was Maplewood Park, where we turned in to eat our lunch, which consisted of tuna fish salad sandwiches on white, pre-sliced ("*goyische*") bread, hard-boiled eggs, a thermos of milk, cookies. Once we had eaten these delicacies, we resumed our journey.

The building was plain, with a matter-of-fact sign announcing "Rochester Public Library, Lake Avenue Branch." However, inside, all was solemn, hushed, with mixed scents of oak and wax polish, the near-religious aura of book-filled rooms. Looking back now, after having had a career as a Renaissance historian and having studied in many of the world's great libraries, I see the Lake Avenue library as the most wonderful, the most important in my life. At a central desk, a gracious lady, sensing the awesomeness of the occasion, handed me the precious library card with a slight flourish. The first three books I chose (prophetically, it seems now) remain vivid in my memory: a book of fairy tales with black and white drawings of men and women in Elizabethan doublets and tights; Abbie Farwell's *John of the Woods*, the story of an orphaned boy in the Middle Ages brought up by monks; Luigi Capuana's *Nimble Legs*, about an Italian boy who was a fast runner and became a messenger for Giuseppe Garibaldi, the great nineteenth-century Italian nationalist.

Between ages eleven and twelve I read, among other novels, *The Three Musketeers*, *The Man in the Iron Mask*, *The Scarlet Pimpernel*, *Captain Blood*, and *The Count of Monte Cristo*. In my teens, I ventured to the Central Library downtown and graduated from historical romance to romantic realism: Nordhoff and Hall's *Falcons of France*, *Mutiny on the Bounty*, *Pitcairn's Island*. From there, it was an easy step to the chronicler-novelists of World War I. I suffered the anguish of Dos Passos' *Three Soldiers*, the carnage of Barbusse's *Under Fire*, the cruel ironies of Humphrey Cobb's *Paths of Glory*, and brooded over the deaths of the disillusioned schoolboys of Remarque's *All Quiet on the Western Front*. These too were prophetic. In the family bookcase, I found Tolstoy's *Resurrection* and Dostoevsky's

Crime and Punishment, and soon began to grasp that there were levels of understanding I had yet to reach.

After school, kids listened to the radio serials, *Tom Mix*, *Little Orphan Annie*, and in the evening, *Dangerous Paradise* and *Chandu the Magician*. On Sundays, the whole family sat around the living room radio to laugh with Eddie Cantor, Fred Allen, and Jack Benny—and, as war approached, to worry over the rapid-fire rantings of Walter Winchell, the Jewish Broadway gossip columnist turned anti-Hitler crusader. On Saturdays, my father tuned in to broadcasts of the Metropolitan Opera; and, on Sundays, dozing off over the Sunday edition of the *Vorverts*—the great Yiddish daily—he listened to the Ford Music Hour.

Thanks to him, music became my second love, next to books. This too had its ethnic tinge: I listened as he periodically recited the roster of great Jewish violinists and pianists and told of having worked in the same New York tailor shop with one Perlmuth, father of the great tenor Jan Peerce and father-in-law of another, Richard Tucker. Tucker, he said, began his great music career as a cantor. Synagogue music and the relative merits of the cantors who sang the Shabbos (sabbath) and High Holidays services was much discussed by my father and his friends. All spoke in awe of Jossele Rosenblatt, "the greatest cantor of all time," whom some of them had heard in New York or at least on recordings.

A year ahead of me in school was Albert Salkowitz, the son of Rochester's most respected cantor. Albert had a fine tenor voice and was being groomed to become a cantor too. Having mastered the falsetto tremor and the glottal sob that were required cantorial techniques, he sometimes took his father's place in our synagogue services. But we his schoolmates knew Albert as a mimic who did outrageously comic impersonations in our high school assemblies, and we had a hard time mustering the proper degree of reverence when we heard him emoting in *shul* (synagogue).

My mother did not share my father's love of music, dismissing the soprano voices on the Saturday morning Met broadcasts as "*kvitchying*"—high-pitched screaming. Still, she believed a well-brought-up boy should be able "to play something." All efforts to introduce me to piano failed. (My father had bought a used piano, which stood in our living room, silently mourning the departure years before of my sister Pearl, the only player in the family.) When my school offered music lessons at very low rates, my mother pressed me to name my instrument. I chose the trumpet; it had a martial character that appealed to me, while the violin seemed overly delicate, and the cello, held between the legs, seemed too gross. So, trumpet it was.

We bought a fairly dent-free used model for twenty dollars. Every Saturday morning, I rode the bus across town with my trumpet case for a half-hour lesson with Miss Jean Smith. With neither passion nor aptitude, and no inclination to practice, I made a sorry pupil. Nevertheless, Mr. Van Heusen, our school's music director, was hard up for players for the Junior High Orchestra, so I was drafted. After one or two practice sessions in which I blundered my solo parts, he saw his mistake. Even my mother came to see that I was hopeless and admitted defeat. I was allowed to stop my lessons, and we sold the instrument to another family with musical aspirations. Still, though I would never have believed it then, the trumpet was, in an odd way, to be in my future,

Neither my father nor his brothers, or any of his friends fit any of the Jewish stereotypes that Hitler was so skillfully and effectively exploiting at the time; none of them was rich, powerful, conspiratorial, communist, avaricious, or stridently ambitious. Rather, they were shopkeepers, barbers, furniture and dry goods salesmen, tailors, clothing pressers, sewing machine operators, and pattern cutters. My gentle Uncle Louie was a wallpaper hanger and house painter. A few who could read and write English well enough might become insurance agents, trudging their neighborhood routes to collect weekly fifty-cent and dollar life insurance premiums from housewives with families much like their own.

The American-born father of my friend Bobby Ribner was a trolley motorman whose great achievement was to make the transition to bus driver. Seymour Stiller's father was a foreman for Bond's, the huge clothing factory that had drawn thousands of Jewish and Italian immigrants to the city.

My father, Harris, (Anglicized, somehow, from Avram Zvi) was a ladies' tailor. Born in the 1880s in a *shtetl* near Minsk, the eldest son of a tenant farmer, he was apprenticed to a *kep* (cap) maker, but ran away to America in 1905 after being called up for the Tsar's army, which was then mobilizing for Russia's disastrous war with Japan. In New York, he found a job in a sweatshop on the lower East Side and learned the tailor's trade. Later, as a married man with six children, he moved to Rochester, where together with a brother-in-law, Hyman Katzowitz, he opened a women's custom suit and coat shop on Clinton Avenue. Their business rode the 1920s wave of prosperity, but crashed with it in 1930. He and Hymie fell out and never spoke to each other again.

Hymie opened his own shop on Clinton Avenue and eventually did well. My father, unable to accept that his irascibility, stubbornness, and innate suspiciousness made him unfit for that kind of intimate association, formed a partnership with his younger brother Sol, and opened a shop, also on Clinton Avenue. That business also foundered on the rocks of economic depression and incompatible temperaments. Hymie, Harris, and Sol, each in his own shop, were now lined up in a row on Clinton Avenue, each a few doors down from the other, where each could compare, disparage, and covertly envy the prosperity of his competitor—even though, until the late 1930s, there wasn't much prosperity to envy. (I recall my father complaining as he returned home one Friday afternoon that "not even a dog" (pronouncing the word as "dug") had come through his door that week.)

Not only did the brothers and brothers-in-law become lifelong strangers to one another, the split-ups inevitably discomposed their families as well. Living in the same neighborhoods, shepherding their children to the same schools, and attending the same synagogues, they inevitably succumbed to gossip, invidious comparisons, rivalries, and strains. We children observed all this and put it down to old-country ways that had no place in our progressive American lives. Refusing to be pulled into their quarrels, we grew up as friends.

If our fathers were not completely American, neither were they like the heroes of the novels I was devouring. Sol and Hymie, and Seymour's father were pale, bespectacled, and wiry. Harris was short and soft-fleshed. All of them were round-shouldered and stiff of movement, although they used their hands gracefully for work and talk. Unlike my friend Davie

Morris's American-born dad, they didn't know how to catch a ball, and were barely aware of the Rochester Red Wings, our hometown baseball team; although Uncle Louie, younger than my father, and a World War I veteran, could talk to you a bit about the team's ups and downs. They did not have man-to-man talks with us the way Andy Hardy did with his father the Judge, in the movies. We called our fathers "Pa," never "Dad" or "Father." Every day except Saturday, at work and at home, they were in shirt sleeves, vests unbuttoned, cuffs folded back to their forearms, ties loosened. They labored long hours, took their meals at the kitchen table (dinners of thick vegetable, barley, lentil, or bean soup, pot roast cooked within an inch of its life, and canned peas and carrots—all washed down with tap water or seltzer, and followed by peaches or pineapple, also from the can).

In our house, after reciting the Friday night *kiddush*, the Sabbath blessing with the prayer over kosher wine, we dined on gefilte fish, chicken soup with *knaydlach* (dumplings), and roast chicken, my mother serving us and fretting when my father complained—as invariably he did—that the soup lacked salt or was not hot enough, or the *knaydlach* were not as good as last week's. We ate the cold leftovers of this dinner the next day, Shabbos, when all labor, including using stoves and turning on lights, was forbidden. Sundays followed an unvarying ritual. We had our big meal at noon, my mother serving her specialties—a thick, bracing cabbage soup or hot beet borscht, followed by a breaded veal chop or, for an occasional treat, a steak cooked unmercifully in the kosher manner. After that, Pa's nap, then a drive in the country which served two of his loves, getting behind the wheel of his pride and joy, a black

Graham Page sedan (succeeded, in time, by a black Oldsmobile sedan) and driving to "the country" to enjoy a still largely unspoiled landscape from the car window. I liked those excursions too. My mother and father were more at peace with each other, and the car was filled with something like good humor. However, as I grew into my teens, the trips came to seem tame and boring. I made my excuses, as Edie and Rose had done before me, and left them to themselves, while I chased more exciting pleasures.

Since school, sports, movies, novels and bike riding were not parts of our parents' world, the range of dinner table topics we could discuss was limited. When I saw my father in animated conversation as he walked to and from *shul* with his friends, I was amazed that they had so much to talk about. They spoke in Yiddish, of course. Most of them read little English, getting their news and opinions from the *Vorverts* and the more Americanized *Jewish Morning Journal*, or, in those days, the radio—although my father also scanned the local paper's headlines every day to make out of its English what he could.

The radio was Pa's second proudest possession. First he bought a shortwave Stromberg Carlson table model, then a huge Philco, with its angled panel and giant dial offering "No Squat, No Stoop, No Squint" convenience. Our first refrigerator was also occasion for great excitement. When Mr. Hyde, our iceman, learned that we had bought one, he sighed, "You should from it have *nachas* (pleasure), but the ones who make them—they should croak!" Since I was the one who had to supplement Mr. Hyde's deliveries by fetching blocks of ice with my cart from Mr. Heckelman's icehouse, my own satisfaction was unalloyed.

Pa was typical of Eastern European immigrants in having had little incentive or opportunity to go to school when he arrived in America. Making a living for a rapidly expanding family was all-consuming, and he hadn't needed to pass any literacy tests to gain the American citizenship that he prized so highly. (He paid his taxes dutifully and considered it his obligation to vote in all elections.) Later, when he would have had the leisure to study English, he was too proud to acknowledge his deficiency. He preferred to weed and plant in his backyard garden, tending to his irises, peonies, lilac trees, carrots, tomatoes, and cucumbers; his father had instilled a love of the earth in him during his boyhood on the family farm. But also from his father, he had learned Hebrew and the habit of Orthodox study. I had neither the language—nor, truth to tell—the interest for it. Still, I carry with me the image of him at the kitchen table, poring nightly over biblical and Talmudic texts.

Back then, our parents had dinned into us that the gentile world was full of dangerous anti-Semites, who had plotted Czarist pogroms and now Hitlerian Nuremberg Laws. (We hadn't yet heard about the death camps.) Still scraping the mud of unpaved *shtetl* streets off their shoes, they were experts on *goyische* hatred. Indeed, it had followed them even to America, their exalted haven. Newspapers and radio broadcasts almost daily carried reports of the latest libels of Father Coughlin and Gerald L.K. Smith, two vocal hyper-Christian commentators, and the crude racism of Senator Bilbo of Mississippi. Joey Bauman, a Catholic playmate from across the street, would taunt me about being a Christ-killer and made fun of my mother's accent. ("What did she say? What did she say?" he would ask in derisive amusement.)

When, at fourteen, I started caddying at the all-wasp Lakeshore Country Club, toting the heavy golf club bags—eighteen holes for a buck—my coworkers found diversion in baiting perhaps the only Jewish caddy they had ever seen. In the caddy fold, where we waited for the call to shoulder a golfer's bag, Caddy Master Freddy Purchase would call out my name: "Wein . . . stein? One of our Irish contingent, eh?" "Yes," I would answer flatly, trying not to engage him. But, his weak joke was the cue for a round of abuse from the other caddies: Aha! I was one of those greedy kikes and thieving yids; or Hitler had the right idea; or some other vicious insult that their communal laughter somehow convinced them was an objective observation or respectable opinion.

I rebutted as best I could, first tentatively, then, warming to the battle, vehemently, countering with racial insults of my own. I would call them drunken Irishmen and stupid Polacks, all too dumb to do anything but carry golf bags for hours in the hot sun for peanuts, resenting Jews because we were smarter and more successful. It gave me a heady feeling, while my antagonists soon tired of the sport and left me alone. Many years later I drove my wife to the Lake Shore Country Club to show her where I had fought my first battle against racism. I parked the car and marched toward the first tee, determined to stand at this bastion of prejudice and segregation and to yell out "Fuck You!" But as I got closer, my resolve melted away. A foursome was approaching from the other side, intent on teeing off. Two of the golfers were black.

Jewishness runs as a scratchy thread among the strands of my American personality. Born and formed in the USA, my buddies and I vaunted our American lingo, American clothes,

American haircuts, American sports, American indifference to tradition, while our old-country parents looked on with resigned acceptance and grudging admiration. We wore our self-doubt on the inside, like a hair shirt made bearable only with laughter and self-mockery. Like all adolescent Americans, we craved excitement and tested limits. We sneaked family cars out of garages and raced them on country roads, sampled our fathers' whiskey, smoked their cigarettes, and bluffed our way past skeptical doormen into betting joints and professional crap games.

Itching with lust, we ogled mature women discreetly, necked with girlfriends possessively, and petted with a few of them timidly. As we approached graduation, we took our sexual gratification where we found it, sometimes with *shiksas*, non-Jewish girls who, so went the myth, at least—were less fussy about chastity than "nice Jewish girls." (Athletes with good physiques appeared to have the edge, whatever their ethnicity, but I, tall, skinny and clumsy at sports, was not one of those.) Still, while our parents might deplore our American wildness and worry about our seemingly inexorable progress toward assimilation, we were intensely, uneasily, proudly, sometimes belligerently, Jewish.

Claiming freedom and equality as our birthright, we found most of our friends among other Jews. That meant Eastern European Jews. German-American Jewry was beyond our ken. The Aresty, a large Sephardic family from Macedonia that moved into our neighborhood, was never fully accepted by our parents as Jewish. They spoke an incomprehensible language and worshiped at a separate synagogue. My father even questioned whether they were really Jews. We in the fourth grade readily integrated their son Jerry, but gave him the affectionately derisive epithet "the Turk." We played baseball and football on urban lots and basketball in the gym of the JY, the Jewish Young Men's and Women's Association, with teammates and rivals who were mirror images of our Jewish-American selves.

English was our native language, but our "mother tongue" was Yiddish. No matter that few of us could speak it very well; Yiddish—or a hyphenated Yiddish-American lingo—furnished us with words and gestures and gave intonation and point to our jokes, our style of conversation, and our debates. We consumed American and English books, but the stories and novels some of us went on to write usually featured Jewish protagonists coming of age in America. In school and at after-school jobs, we mingled with non-Jews, but we seldom formed close friendships across that line.

I can't think about my family apart from its *shtetl*-flavored Jewishness. For a long time, I thought there could be no family as strange and embarrassing as mine, and I was as secretive about it as I was able to be. Now I see that even its strangeness was peculiarly Jewish. I was the fruit of a misconceived union between an immigrant spinster and a much older immigrant widower with six children. Desperate to escape the drudgery of a New York sweatshop and the shame of being an old maid, my mother Rayzel (Anglicized as Rose) allowed herself to be matched up with Harris by Mrs. Mentor, a Rochester lady who was an amateur *shadchin*, or marriage broker.

I guess my mother regarded Mrs. Mentor as a benefactor. Whenever she announced we were going to visit her, I wanted to hide. I hated Mrs. Mentor's stiff mission oak furniture and the stuffy, antiquated smell of her place. I hated the way she pinched my cheek and addressed me in whining baby talk. I was frightened by her neighbor, a developmentally disabled girl who always seemed to be there whenever we visited. Underlying it all, as I realized even then, was my resentment against Mrs. Mentor for being the architect of my parents' unhappiness and my unease.

Family life was an emotional minefield. My father's first wife had died (so I learned much later) when she took it upon herself to abort a seventh pregnancy. What resentments this created toward my father, what remorse he himself nursed, I never knew. What I did know were the tensions produced in the household by Pa's trigger temper as he directed it at the shortcomings of one or another member of the family. Nor did my mother bring any peace into the equation; unable to cope with her husband's moods, browbeaten by him, and un-motherly toward her stepchildren, she lavished her affection on me—and I squirmed under it.

My two oldest half-brothers, Izzy and George soon left. I later learned that Izzy's departure came after a fistfight with my father, ostensibly over a disputed camera. Sarah went to New York to live with Eva, her mother's well-to-do sister, and became Sally. She found a job as secretary to a high-powered executive on the New York Produce Exchange. (We heard he made $7500 a year!) Eventually, Sally married Deni Sinsheimer, a refugee from Nazi Germany who, we were told, came from a distinguished family. The marriage was another tug away from the family's wholly Eastern European origins. Sally's suicide a few years later, in some confused way, seemed to legitimize our misgivings about relations with German Jews.

Pearl, the next oldest, had a good job as head stenographer at Clapp's Baby Food Company and continued to live at home. Pearl was as tough as Pa and gave as good as she got. Her marriage to Polish-born Sam Maron, shortly to receive his Ph.D. in physical chemistry from Columbia, made all of us very proud. Even though, in 1937, Pa's business had barely begun to recover, he spared no expense to host a dinner and wedding in his cherished garden. Rose, the middle sibling, lacked the gene for tact and had what we called a "big mouth"; and, because she lacked Pearl's aggressive strength, she took the most heat from Pa. Edie and I, the two youngest, tended to stay out of the line of fire, although once when I came to my mother's defense against Pa's verbal abuse, he rounded on me, and I retreated.

Still, early on, I became aware that my much-feared father himself lived in fear, that having been born and grown to young manhood beyond the pale, and having run away to America to escape war, poverty, and pogroms, he perceived the world as a dangerous and hostile place. The anger and alarm he vented on his family and the violence he threatened (but never delivered) were his way of dealing with those fears. Sudden noises—the clang of a pot cover falling to the floor startled him into fury, as did a lamp left lighted or a dripping faucet. Those who committed such domestic crimes felt the sharp edge of his tongue. But he reserved his scabrous language for people outside the family and usually employed it on the telephone, for example, to business and service people with whom he had had some dispute over a charge or a faulty product: "Mr., you, you... should stick your nose in hell!" or, "Mr., you should live, but not long!" And of an absent antagonist: *"A zamin bestid-- soll er shtinken von halz!"* ("That bastard, a foul smell should come from his throat." The Yiddish word for bastard was "*momser*," but that usually had an affectionate connotation. "*Bestid*" was more in the spirit he intended.)

My father and his sister, Aunt Pauline, known as Paulie, fought an ongoing war that was interrupted by precarious truces, during which the families were much in each other's houses. Although, as a child, I simply took their feud as a fact of life—the product of two equally quarrelsome natures—as I grew older and more observant, I began to suspect that a deep grievance gnawed at them and kept their anger alive. I never learned what it was, although I suspected it had to do with Paulie's involvement in the fatal abortion.

When the truce was on, Sunday afternoons and evenings were often spent at my aunt's house. Most family visits were tedious for me—nothing but grown-up talk—but at Aunt Paulie's, I was allowed to rummage for treasures in their hall closet, and I could always persuade Uncle Jake to play his cornet. Paulie was one of the few women in our family who drove a car and, on hot summer days, she sometimes took my mother, Edie, Rose, and me to the public beach at Charlotte on Lake Ontario. When the feud resumed, as it inevitably did, our houses were off-limits, and we were denied those pleasures.

Whether there was a secret grievance or not, Aunt Paulie shared my father's appetite for combat and at least some of his paranoia. She had a nose for smelling offence, carried long-term grudges, and cultivated the well-turned insult; my mother was a favorite target, mainly on account of her frumpiness and her lowly position in the pecking order. She called my Aunt Anna, who had come from Warsaw as a young woman to marry my uncle Sol, die Greeneh, the Greenhorn. The slur was taken up by all the sisters-in-law, although this particular greenhorn was more beautiful and stylish than they, the only one who could read English and American newspapers and books, play bridge, and follow what was going on in what we called "the entertainment world."

Anna also proved to be very spunky. When Uncle Sol died, leaving her with three small children and little money, she got a job on a sewing machine at Bond's. A few years later, while I was waiting to be called up for military service, I worked as a "floor boy" in the same shop, pushing a hand cart on which I piled overcoat parts and moved them along from assemblers to button-holers to pressers. Anna and I formed a lasting friendship. Many years later, not long before she died, her engineer son Norman brought her to visit me and my new bride. I had just published a book and quietly placed a copy in her lap. Anna turned it over, looked inside, and glowing with pleasure, murmured in her Polish English, "This is vat ve struggled for."

As the only child of my doting, fussing, harried, and nervous mother, I was more protected and less frequently criticized than my sisters, although I was the cause of the most acute paternal disappointment. On Rosh Hashonah, Yom Kippur, Passover, and other important holidays, I was condemned to spend hours at my father's side in *shul*. (He had given up trying to compel my attendance every week on Shabbos.) While my mother in her holiday finery looked down at us from the crowded women's gallery, helpless to protect me from my father's embarrassingly loud reproofs, (some of which could be heard above the din of chanting), I struggled to recite the Hebrew prayers which I had mumbled three times every week for many years under the strained but less vocal supervision of

Mr. Shatz, my Hebrew teacher. (Once, after I had kicked Mr. Shatz in the shins as he tried to intercept me in the street and edge me into his apartment for my lesson, he took his grievance—and his bruises—to my father, and there was hell to pay.)

The *shul* was hot and stuffy. The wooden benches were straight-backed and hard, and the place smelled of tobacco, snuff, the yellowing paper of dusty prayer books, stale breath, shoe polish, shaving lotion, and sweat—the amalgam that I came to think of as the authentic flavor of orthodox piety. Later, on visits home, after I had begun to take religion more seriously, I accompanied my father to *shul* on Saturdays. I also went fishing with him, an occasional pastime he took up in retirement. But still later, when I wrote from Italy to tell him and my mother that I was marrying a *shiksa*, he was crushed. However, he swallowed his anger and made plans to greet us when we returned, perhaps softened by the news that my wife was pregnant. Sadly, before we arrived to show him his first grandson, he had died of a heart attack. By that time, my religious ardor had cooled, but I started going to afternoon services to recite the *Kaddish*, the mourner's prayer, for him, and this drew me back into the fold. "Well, he won!" I told myself. But even then I knew it was only a temporary victory.

If Pa had been exasperated by my ineptitude in Hebrew, he was positively contemptuous of my skinny, angular body. In his eyes I would be too weak to meet life's challenges—perhaps those threatened from the ubiquitous anti-Semites. As he used to put it, "You vouldn't be able to hoit a fly." This inadequacy was most likely to come to his attention at meal times, since he thought that it was due to my lack of appetite for my mother's cooking. While he shoveled in mountains of food at each meal, I appeared barely to pick at my plate, particularly falling short in my consumption of bread, considered almost reverently in our family as the staff of life. "Oy, er esst ohn broit!" (Oh, he's eating without bread!), they would say. My mother's between-meal offerings of fruit or cookies I usually rejected as a way of asserting my independence and also of showing solidarity with my sisters, who generally were not offered the same treats. Actually, as I entered my teens, I developed an enormous appetite, and unbeknownst to my parents, was wolfing down hamburgers, barbecued beef sandwiches, and thick hot dogs—all *traif,* or non-kosher—on nightly jaunts about town with my friends.

At thirteen, six feet tall, and growing, I accompanied my five-foot-five father to the *shul* to chant my *maftir,* the Torah commentary assigned to the bar-mitzvah boy, and to deliver my prepared speech, the same one recited by all the pupils of Mr. Shatz, who had composed, translated, and typed it out in multiple copies. ("My dear parents, ladies and gentlemen, today I am a man . . . .") First, though, my father presented me to old Rabbi Solomon Sadowski, who, although I did not know it then, was a distinguished Hassidic scholar and author. From his usual seat beside the *bimah,* the altar platform, the Rebbe looked up at me from above his spectacles as though he were seeing me for the first time. After a brief perusal, he said to my father, "Ein shainer Jung"—a good-looking boy. "Yeh," replied my father, "awber er esst nit."(Yes, but he doesn't eat!).

2.

FRONT STREET FOLLIES

A t sixteen, my part-time work changed from caddying at the country club, hawking peanuts at the Elks' weekly amateur fights, and jerking sodas in Manny's Drug Store to selling new and used clothes at Sol Goldstein's Front Street Clothing Market. Front Street had been the earliest center of Jewish commercial and religious life in Rochester. When Jewish immigrants first arrived in the city in numbers in the mid-nineteenth century, they gravitated toward Front Street, on the edge of the river, near the main business district. They opened clothing stores and tailoring shops, and their first *shul*. Those shops were the forerunners of the great men's clothing factories; Bond's, Hickey Freeman, Michael Stern, and Timely Clothes are the best known of these brands. These factories, together with strictly wasp Eastman Kodak and German-flavored Bausch and Lomb, transformed Rochester from a way station on the Erie Canal into a major industrial city.

By the 1930s, the successful Jewish industrialists had long since outgrown their cramped quarters on Front Street, and had built their factories and synagogues elsewhere. After this shift, Front Street deteriorated to a few dingy blocks of pawnshops, second-hand clothing stores, a couple of rowdy saloons, one or two food wholesalers (among whom was my neighborhood friend Harold Newell's father), a poultry merchant, and a smoke shop. The smoke shop was one of the few non-Jewish enterprises on the street. It was run by a mysterious Italian-American named Mikey Troy, who wrapped his hands in sinister-looking black-bandages and pulled a Panama hat down low on his head. The rumor was that he wore his hat this way to cover the disfigurement suffered when some of his enemies "took him for a ride." The story was that it had something to do with the illegal betting on horse races and baseball games he presided over in the back room. Besides the gamblers and bargain hunters who were the mainstay of its economy, the street's regulars were panhandlers, drunks, and gawkers. A phlegmatic Irish foot patrolman armed with a revolver and a billy club watchfully kept his eye over all.

In going to work for Sol Goldstein, I was uncomfortably aware that I was entering the disreputable world of the Jewish hustler. But the pay was good, and the job, in its own way, meant more responsibility than any of my previous jobs— and it was more fun. Sol was a curly-haired, medium-sized, middle-aged man, whose sallow complexion, red-rimmed eyes, and incipient paunch betrayed a chronic lack of fresh air and exercise. (In his younger days, he had been an avid baseball player, but money-making had left him no time for sports.) Sol's intense, wary expression could give way to a broad grin if he heard a funny or off-color story, or to a furtive smile if he sensed that a transaction was going his way. A shrewd and creative dealmaker, Sol was probably the most successful merchant on a street on which the primary imperative was "Get what you can!"

Behind its cluttered display windows and blinking neon sign, Sol's store was jammed with racks of cheap new and second-hand men's suits, overcoats, and pants, shelves of dress shirts, neckties, socks, underwear, jeans (called "dungarees" in those days), and denim work shirts, jackets, and gloves. On a balcony toward the rear of the store (which, like all the buildings on that side of Front Street, hung its backside out over the Genesee River), boxes of footwear—dress shoes, work boots, galoshes, and rubbers—were stacked to the ceiling. Also on offer were fishing tackle and hunting gear and caps, and anything else Sol thought he could sell at a profit. Customers came to Front Street looking for deals they thought they could not get in the more fashionable shops on Main Street and Clinton Avenue, and the regulars knew that Sol's prices were flexible.

In a typical negotiation, we salesmen would draw from a wide repertoire of sales pitches:

"Whaat? You don't like this cloth? But this is dreck from Paris!"

"It's pre-War goods; the price is a steal!"

"Shhh! Take it before the boss finds out and fires me!"

"Today is a Jewish holiday, so we're selling everything at a special bargain price!"

"So it's not pure wool! Don't you know there's a war on?"

Meanwhile, Sol would be following the banter closely from another part of the store and, scarcely moving his mouth, would sometimes intervene with directions to us in Yiddish:

"Nem die gelt!" (Take the money!) or "Loz im gehen!" (Let him walk).

It was Sol's guiding principle that everyone who turned onto Front Street (excepting the drunks) was a potential customer; the trick was to get him inside his shop. He and his competitors (including his half-brother Harry Wolin, who owned a similar store next door, his mother, who had a tiny used goods shop a few doors down, and his uncle Sawatsky, who was in the same line at the other end of the street) employed "pullers" to stand in front of their establishments in all but the most miserable weather—welcoming, cajoling, hustling, and using any other means short of brute force, to persuade passers-by to come through their doors. In her men's work shoes and housewife's apron and babushka, Sol's mother was her own puller. Sawatsky's front man was his son Abie. Abie was a squat, stiff-legged, and scowling fellow, whose pulled-down fedora, dark, double-breasted suits, and side-of the mouth lingo—all in imitation his Jewish gangster model, Edgar G. Robinson—made him seem much older than his years. (He was soon to be drafted into what he referred to as "dat der Army.")

Sol's puller was Jack Cohen, alias Jake the Meatball, a tall, well-formed man of about forty, with reddish-blond hair and a matching Buffalo Bill mustache. With his broad brimmed felt hat and luxuriant double-breasted camel's hair overcoat, he cut a handsome, imposing figure. Jake welcomed every potential customer with a smile and non-stop jovial patter. His heavy New York City accent fascinated them and kept his fellow employees laughing. How he had come by his nickname we never learned, although his suave and slightly conspiratorial style suggested a racy, possibly shady, history. This suspicion was reinforced when his brother George showed up at the store one day. Jake welcomed him and persuaded Sol to take him on as a part-time salesman, but his guarded enthusiasm suggested that brother George was part of a past he was trying to forget.

George was a big man too, but where his brother radiated geniality, he glowered and swaggered, and his humor was rougher. While Jake had settled into conventional domestic life with his hefty wife and two young daughters, (a little family that occasionally had me over to dinner in their small apartment just off Joseph Avenue, the hub of Rochester's Jewish community), George was unattached when he arrived, although he soon married a local woman, a bookkeeper in a small business firm. Apparently, George persuaded her to skim off some money from her employers. Once caught and charged, she implicated George, and both were convicted. George was sent to prison for a couple of years. She was let off with a suspended sentence and probation. We thought that remarkably just.

Sol's other full-time employee was Mr. Eber. (If he had a first name, no one knew what it was, and he was never addressed in any other way.) Mr. Eber was a tiny septuagenarian, always dressed in the same ancient brown suit, who, in his snuffling, gap-toothed Yiddish-English, maintained a belligerently profane commentary on the world in general. While he mostly ignored me and my friend Albert, (whom, at my recommendation, Sol had also hired), he viewed us as passing irritants—spoiled, ignorant kids who did not really have to work for a living—requiring no respect from him. For customers, he had only contempt, regarding them as uniformly stupid and there only to be exploited. Mr. Eber's great pleasure was to exchange obscene Yiddish banter with Jake. In one of his grosser witticisms, repeated over and over like a refrain, he would call out, "Jake, Jake, zog mir, von ah putz in tochis kenn man schwengerin?" ("Jake, Jake, tell me, can someone be impregnated by a prick in the ass?") I understood most of the Yiddish, but Albert had to tell me what "schwengerin," meant; in my family becoming pregnant was always spoken of in hushed tones in my presence.

Among the people whom Jake regularly engaged from his station in front of the store was Carl, the city sanitation department worker who collected Front Street's garbage. Carl was simple-minded, with a laugh as huge as his denim-covered girth and a penchant for reciting children's rhymes like Peter Peter, Pumpkin Eater. Carl's wife matched him in size, and Jake loved to tease him about their sex life. This always made Carl giggle in embarrassment and exclaim "Pshaw!," but he never became angry.

Another of Jake's regular interlocutors was Dave Solomon, owner of the pawnshop across the street. Dave seemed to have long before gotten stuck in his wife's family business, despite having been educated for finer things. His age and dignified bearing had earned him the title "Mayor of Front Street." Often, while he waited for potential shoppers to pull in, Jake would banter and joke with Dave across the way. One day, after an altercation with an extremely unsatisfied customer who had nearly destroyed the awning in front of his shop, Dave had been hauled into court and fined a small sum for fighting. As he stood on a ladder ripping down the tattered awning, Jake yelled to him, "Dave, Dave, what are you doing up there?" Without hesitation, Dave yelled back: "I'm making a suit of clothes for the judge!"

Out of Jake the Meatball's New York menagerie, arrived a character called Willy on the Level. Sixtyish, stocky, and with thinning hair, Willy seemed to have earned his nickname from his habit of complaining that people were not "on the level" with him. His hunched shoulders and mournful look—mouth perpetually turned-down at the corners—telegraphed the suspicious air with which he confronted his demons. The story Jake told us was that Willy had gone on the bum after his wife and her lover (Willy's partner) cheated him out of his share of their small Brooklyn trucking business. From time to time, he showed up at Sol's to get Jake's sympathetic ear. Eventually, he found a job in a Rochester factory that was doing war work. But trouble followed Willy even there. He pocketed—perhaps absent-mindedly—a roll of the company's friction tape, and was caught with it as he checked out at the end of his shift. He was arrested and locked in the county jail while awaiting his appearance before a judge. When Albert and I visited him there, he grasped the bars of his cell and called, "Albert, Albert, get me out of here!," looking for all the world like a Jewish Jimmy Cagney on death row. But there was nothing we could do. Willy served his sentence, and then disappeared.

Wartime shortages were hurting Sol's business. As a small shopkeeper who bought up remainders, surplus goods, and used clothing, he was at the lower end of the supply chain. Wholesalers distributed their products to larger and more respectable outlets long before they offered anything to him; at the same time, people were wearing out their clothes instead of selling them on the second-hand market. So, Sol was pressed to find new sources. Eyeing the cheap and still relatively plentiful goods on offer at some more respectable stores, he sent Albert and me to buy up whatever we could get, which he would then resell at a small markup.

One of our sources was a chain shoe store outlet, where rubbers and galoshes were to be had at bargain prices. After we had visited and bought their goods a few times, the manager discovered we were Sol's employees and kicked us out. But we needed our suppliers, so I borrowed Jake's camel hair coat and created a fake mustache. Albert devised a makeshift costume too, and we returned, sometimes separately, sometimes together. But the manager soon recognized us through our disguises and angrily escorted us off the premises, warning us not to come back.

By that time, our careers as undercover men would soon be over anyway. Army service was calling Albert, some months my senior. Sol organized a farewell party for Albert and Abie Sawatsky, who had also received his summons to "dat der Army." He invited Mrs. Sol, Albert, Abie, and me and my girlfriend to a local supper club, as restaurants with Broadway-style entertainment were called. This one featured a band, a dance chorus, and a stand-up comedian named Joey Di Paolo. We knew Joey; he shopped on Front Street for the fancy suits (not unlike Abie's) he wore for his performances and, as he explained, "for when I gotta meet some important people." We were mildly excited to see his show.

Having finished dinner, we were enjoying dessert at our stage-side table just as Joey took the mike. He acknowledged our applause and led off with a joke that was becoming widely popular throughout the country. First he delivered the set-up:

The first American to sink an enemy battleship was Colin Kelly. The first American to land on Guadalcanal was Robert O'Hara. The first woman to lose five sons was named Sullivan.

Then came the punch line:

The first American to apply for a ration card to get new tires for his car was Nathan Goldstein.

Groans of dismay rose from the Sol Goldstein party. Joey heard, and apparently recognized us. He stopped, pretending to be surprised: "What, you didn't like that?" he asked. We mumbled something about being there to celebrate two of our party who were about to enter military service. He seemed to miss the point, and we, embarrassed, made no further protest. Abie and Albert went off to war shortly after that, Albert never to return. As far as I know, Joey continued to tell such jokes to supper club audiences for the rest of the war.

3.

LOVE AND WAR

Growing up in nineteen-thirties America, a Jew, a democrat (and a Democrat), hearing ever more gruesome and bitter accounts of the war in Europe and the Pacific, I could in no way become a pacifist. War against fascist dictators seemed a matter of plain justice and urgent necessity. I first heard of Hitler when I was eight or nine. Walking home from school, Arthur Meltzer told me about the bad German man who hated Jews and blamed them for the world's troubles. At first, I thought this was another of Arthur's inventions. (Bullied by two older brothers, ignored by his father, and browbeaten by his demanding mother, Arthur invented a lot.) But, when on all sides, I began hearing about Hitler and the Nazis, I decided they were real. My father denounced them daily, Germans now nudging out Poles in his mind as the worst Antisemiten. In our house, Hitler was not merely a man's name; it was a collective noun, a judgment bestowed on all those who wished Jews evil. In Yiddish and in English, my father cursed all Hitlers; and my mother, wringing her hands, begged God to protect us against them.

Getting into the war was a burning ambition of my mid-teens; so was getting laid. "Make love *and* war" was my motto. When Pearl Harbor was bombed, I was only fifteen and ago-nizingly remote from both. Bobby Ribner and I made a pact to enlist in the Marines when we turned seventeen in 1943, he in February, I in March. Together, we hoped, we might be able to persuade our parents to give their consent. But Bobby died of a kidney ailment just before his seventeenth birthday; and, without having him to present as a model, I was too timid to face my father's certain anger and my mother's teary panic. Almost another year of marching in place went by. I passed the written exam for the Navy V-12 program, but flunked the vi-sion test, too near-sighted to read the small letters on the chart. So I was back to waiting until my eighteenth birthday, when I would be eligible for the draft. With the fighting going in favor of the Allies, I was afraid the War would end before I could get into it.

In the battle against virginity, though—after many frus-trated sorties—inglorious victory was mine at last. Well, it was at least a sort of victory. Ken Goldstein, a year ahead of me in high school, knew of a whorehouse and, better yet, knew how to get admitted into it. One summer evening, Ken, Davie Morris, and I sallied forth to find the place. You entered the Dew Drop Inn, a rundown false-front restaurant on Hudson Avenue, walked directly and purposefully to the back door and out into the yard. You climbed a rickety stairway and knocked at the door on the landing. At your knock, a tough-looking woman opened the door a crack and asked what you wanted.

After she had answered our knock, and Ken had told her why we were there, she was satisfied that we were not cops but only horny kids. She then led us into a parlor, took a seat, and motioned for us to do likewise. A young woman in a bathrobe and slippers was seated on a sagging sofa, watching a little boy playing on the rug. "I'm not working tonight," she volunteered. We looked around while we waited, making polite conversation with her and the madam. A few stuffed chairs, some movie magazines, a radio, a glimpse of a kitchen, the child playing at our feet—we might have been at a neighbor's house respectably taking tea instead of sitting in a den of iniquity awaiting our turn to fornicate. Ken went first and emerged in about ten minutes looking blanched. I faltered, but before I could back out, I was told it was my turn.

A tall, handsome, broad-shouldered woman in a flowery kimono, with a black pageboy haircut, summoned me to follow her down a hallway. The room we entered contained a dresser, a bed, and a night stand with a basin. She said her name was Dolores, held out her hand for my five dollars, peeled off her robe, and stood before me, suddenly, startlingly, matter-of-factly, naked. With massive breasts, broad pale red-nipples, full-hips, and a firm, shapely ass, she was the first woman ever to make herself naked for me. She watched me struggle with my belt buckle and zipper, stumble out of my pants, and pull off my shorts. When she took hold of my hesitant member to sponge it off with the dingy pink liquid in the bedside basin that, I later learned, was standard equipment in whorehouses, I blurted out that this was my first time. I guess I was hoping for some special consideration with this sudden confession, but she was almost contemptuous, looking up and scoffing, "Christ, a cherry!" Then she lay on her back on the bed, parted her legs and summoned me. "Leave the tits alone!" she warned as I attempted to stroke her breasts (more to arouse myself than her). Waving off the condom I was shakily trying to put on, she took me in hand and guided my fumbling incompetence to a quick, official conclusion.

The next time I visited the Dew Drop Inn, Dolores, the other women, and the little boy were nowhere to be seen. Instead, the only person I encountered was a slender blonde woman in a housecoat vacuuming the rugs. She switched off the machine and led me into the same bedroom where she repeated Dolores' routine: told me her name (Rita), snatched up my fiver, stripped, washed me with the pink solution, and then stretched out on the bed. This time I was ready for her frank and businesslike nakedness and performed with more assurance. After Rita, I found other prostitutes, some white, some black. The most sordid of these couplings took place in the least likely of settings. A broken-nosed, heavy-set man about my father's age, who looked more like a coal hauler than a pimp, appropriately kept a woman in a neighborhood coal bin.

He ushered me in, took my money, and went outside to wait until I finished. The woman—white, no longer young, dumpy, with frizzy-hair and a mouth smeared with red lipstick—didn't give me her name, but she was chatty, almost motherly. As she wiped me down with the pink liquid, she kept up a running commentary on the moral ills of the times, especially decrying all those girls who nowadays were "giving it away free." Then, raising her skirt to her waist (in this semifrigid cellar the clothes stayed on), she took a gob of Vaseline from a jar, lubricated her not-so-private parts, joking that she had to grease the cat, and invited me to climb on top of her on her dingy cot. Afterward, emboldened by her talkativeness, I asked her how she had become a hooker. She gave this witless question the explanation it deserved, one no doubt rehearsed in retellings to the legion of inquisitive men who had preceded me to the coal bin: as a young innocent girl, she had been ruined by an older man ("he took my cherry"); and, thus, shunned by respectable society, she had turned to selling "it." The descent into the coal bin was not hard to imagine.

Sex was like a drug to me; it always left me wanting more. (War, as I was later to learn, was not like that at all.) But, despite the coal bin lady's complaint, those girls who were giving it away for free were hard to find. Yet it did seem that women were becoming more available to us. The perception probably also reflected our own coming of age. Taller, more experienced, more self-confident, we were becoming sexually more interesting to women. We were also enjoying the benefits of wartime mores. Men were scarce, and women were willing to take previously unthinkable risks to find male companionship. Inhibitions were relaxed, and conventions put on hold, if not permanently discarded. Strangers struck up conversations, made contacts in bars, and even introduced themselves on the street. Military uniforms gave their wearers an edge, but we civilians were more consistently available. We sharpened our skills and became adept at the art of the pick-up and the quick seduction.

As my friends and I ranged further afield to find women, we were always worried that, because we were Jews, gentile girls would rebuff us. We used fake names (my *nom de corse* being Donald Weston) and told as many lies as we needed to maintain the deception. Dishonesty worked to a degree, but we kept these encounters brief, lest we give ourselves away with a careless word, or be given away by an unwitting friend hailing us in the street with our real names. When such things happened, the break was sharp and the embarrassment great. At Critic's, the coffee shop where my friends and I hung out after school, I once made a date with Lorraine, one of the waitresses who worked there. On the evening of our date, a Friday, I went to her apartment and, after a few awkward preliminaries, we had sex on her sofa. We agreed we would go out together the next night. At 7:30 I presented myself, all smug confidence, at Lorraine's door, a bouquet of flowers in hand. She opened the door and seemed surprised to see me. Behind her was a man, also dressed as for a night on the town. Warily eyeing my rival, I reminded her that we had a date, whereupon she cooly informed me that she did not want to see me again. "Why not?" I asked. "Because I can't go out with a Jew." "Wh-what made you think I was a Jew?" I stuttered, mendacious to the end. "Because last night you told me you had chicken for dinner; I got to thinkin': you have ta' be Jewish, because only Jews have chicken on Friday night!" So much for Donald Weston. At sixteen I started "going steady" with a girl named Florence. Her father was a prosperous manufacturer of men's pants and had moved his chubby, genial wife, two daughters, and small son to a spacious house across town, in a neighborhood recently opened to upwardly mobile Jews. Florence's older sister Marilyn was a junior at the University of Michigan (one of the few good universities that seemed not to have a Jewish quota). To me, Marilyn was glamorous; with her flashy make up, showy clothes, and racy patter, she hinted at levels of worldly experience I could only guess at. Although Florence idolized her, she didn't imitate her.

Florence was petite and well formed, but not as pretty as Marilyn and not as "fast." She marched in the high school band, cheeks puffed out as she sucked on her clarinet, long strawberry blonde hair trailing down from her military cap, short legs encased in wide trousers. Her ambitions went no further than high school graduation, a stint in secretarial school, then an office job to be followed by marriage. Although she was no prude, she carefully protected her market value.

In her darkened living room we necked hour after excruciating hour. In those pre-pill days, the passage from necking (embracing and kissing) to petting (kissing and touching above the waist) to heavy petting (kissing, unlimited touching, stroking and handling) was fraught with emotional, moral, and practical hazards. Florence was a necker, no more, no less. In the dozens of hours we spent tossing about on her family sofa, we never sailed beyond the first barrier. Truth to tell, for the first two years of our "going steady," I didn't even think of testing deeper waters, so pleased was I to have Florence as my girlfriend and so firmly did I subscribe to the double standard. Good girls—certainly Jewish girls, the kind you would marry—did not put out before marriage, or at least, not before becoming formally engaged.

At the same time, Florence understood that my sexual needs extended beyond the Florsheim living room, and she even seemed to take prurient pleasure when I boasted (usually untruthfully) about getting them satisfied elsewhere. She may also have regarded my extra-curricular sexual activity as a safety valve releasing pressures she might otherwise have had to cope with. In time, however, our voyages on the family sofa became more passionate, particularly after I had enlisted in the Army and came home periodically on leave from the Army. Although it was not the reason I had so desperately wanted to get in, the uniform was Aladdin's lamp so far as sex was concerned. I enjoyed its power in Birmingham, Alabama, Atlanta, Georgia, and Augsburg, Germany, and wherever else my military assignments took me, never once wondering whether my conquests got any fraction of the pleasure they were giving me.

When I came home on furlough, Florence and I returned to necking on the living room sofa, but now she let me feel her breasts—without, to be sure, letting me get inside her blouse—then tolerated my rubbing my aroused body against her. When I ventured to throw my leg over her she pushed me away at first, but eventually she let me lie on her and move up and down to simulate intercourse. My friends and I called this "dry humping," but in this case it was a misnomer, since it was not dry. After I had come, I would get up, give myself a perfunctory wipe with my handkerchief, smooth my rumpled uniform, and dash out to catch the last bus home, hoping that the other late night passengers wouldn't notice the large sticky stain seeping through my khaki trousers.

By then wartime uncertainties and delays were moving Florence to reconfigure her timetable, and she wanted me to make a commitment to marriage. This forced me to acknowledge a feeling that had been growing along with my sexual confidence; I did not want to marry Florence—or anyone—either sooner or later; I only wanted to have sex, and since sex with her was not an option, we parted on more or less friendly terms. By happy coincidence, when I returned to camp, I found that my friend Sandy Sarachan had sent me a letter confessing that on *his* last furlough he had fallen in love with Florence, and asking whether it was okay to court her. Magnanimously, I gave him the green light. Six months later, Florence and Sandy were married. I was in Camp Butner, North Carolina and missed the wedding.

4.

DUBBIN

"Can the foot soldier teach anything important about war, having been there? I think not. He can tell wars stories."

Timothy O'Brien, *If I Die in a Combat Zone*

While I was huffing and puffing through basic training at Fort McClellan in Alabama in late November of 1944, I got a letter from my friend Albert Gleiner "somewhere in France." He wrote of being close enough to the Germans to hear them talking to each other, and described getting sprayed with shrapnel that tore up the raincoat that he had left lying on the edge of his foxhole. He recounted his brother Marv's reports of success with the ladies in Paris (all three Gleiner boys had joined the Army), disparaged the rural French women he had seen, and asked me to send chocolate. I bought several boxes at the PX and mailed them to him. A few days later, I got a letter from my girlfriend Florence saying how sorry she was about Albert. I rushed to the PX to call her. She did not know I had not yet received the news: Albert had been killed in action. He never got the chocolates.

After the late-December start of the mighty German counter-offensive in the Ardennes, the allies began calling it the Battle of the Bulge. Every afternoon, once the day's training routines were over, we would assemble in the company street to hear Sergeant Zukauskas read the war bulletins. (He was really only a corporal, but calling him Sergeant made us feel more important, less like raw recruits and more like soldiers.) By late December, new names and places started to appear in the bulletins: Von Runstedt, Jülich, Malmédy, St. Vith, Prüm, Schnee Eifel, Bastogne, General McAuliffe (he who replied "Nuts" to a German demand to surrender his troops surrounded in Bastogne.) Also, we began to hear technical terms unfamiliar to our rookie ears: aircraft visibility, tactical withdrawal, re-groupment, and relief column, among others.

But none of that was very real to us. Our world was the firing range and the mess hall, marches in the heavily forested Talladega Mountains, and preparation for inspection. This meant cleaning the barracks, grooming ourselves according to Army standards, stripping and cleaning M-1s, and rubbing shoes with dubbing—or "dubbin," as we called it. Dubbin was thick, slick, smelly, waterproofing grease that came in a small round olive drab government-issue can—and we hated it. If our noncoms were not browbeating us about keeping our rifle barrels SHINY AS A BABY'S ASS, drawing the blankets on our cots ASSHOLE TIGHT, field-stripping our cigarette butts to make them disappear into the ground, policing the company street (ASSES AND ELBOWS; THAT'S ALL I WANNA SEE; ASSES AND ELBOWS!), cutting our hair down to quarter-inch stubble, then they were nagging, warning, threatening us to KEEP THOSE BOOTS GREASED WITH DUBBIN' AT ALL TIMES! NOT ENOUGH DUBBIN' ON YOUR SHOES! The problem with basic training was not so much the marches in the Alabama heat or the hours on the firing range trying to hit targets you could barely see, but all the chicken shit stuff thrown at you just to convince you that you were under discipline and had to do things the Army way.

The bulletins got worse. The Germans had opened a huge hole in our lines in Belgium and northeastern France, and were aiming for the Meuse River and Antwerp. We were told that our remaining weeks of basic training had been cut from eight to two. We were to go on a three-day bivouac combat simulation exercise, then back to barracks for final cleanup and packing before shipping out. We would have ten-day furloughs before reporting to Camp Kilmer, New Jersey, a port of embarkation. Thirteen weeks of infantry training seemed pretty skimpy, but it was a relief to know that basic training was almost over. The prospect of the real thing was scary but exciting. The Army did not tell us where we were going, but you did not have to be Secretary of War to figure out that the Kilmer POE meant the European theater, or that it was the German counter-attack, the Battle of the Bulge, that had cut our infantry training short. "Good," we thought. None of us wanted to fight the Japanese in some remote Pacific jungle.

At Kilmer, we got new uniforms and equipment, and were formed into "salt water" companies for the ocean journey. On the ship, I was reunited with Murray Blumenthal, a gangly, kinky-haired eighteen-year old from the Bronx I had done basic training with at Fort McClellan. We helped each other endure the overbearing lieutenant who commanded our provisional company, and were happy when, because he had slipped on the December ice and broken his leg, he had been forced to stay behind. We crossed the Atlantic on the Queen Elizabeth, which had been refitted as a troop ship, its frescoed walls protected by plywood sheets, its damask sofas and chairs removed, and its cabins and decks stacked with 13,000 bunks. Besides the similarity of our ages, ethnicity, and body types, Murray and I were natural friends by virtue of what we felt were our special aesthetic and intellectual proclivities. We read a lot and liked to think we were more sensitive than most of our fellow recruits. Murray was a budding professional trombone player drafted out of Julliard, who seemed to me very sophisticated. After a trip of eight or nine days, tracing a serpentine course to avoid U-boats, we docked at Greenock, Scotland under cover of night. Standing at the ship's rail as we approached land, he took my sensibilities to a new level: gazing up at the craggy Scottish mountains hovering over us Murray solemnly intoned, "Now I know what is meant by Old World beauty."

Disembarking to the incomprehensible chatter of Scottish bargemen, we boarded troop trains. As we traveled south, Scotland and England were invisible to us through blacked out windows, and the long hours were broken only by a stop in Lancaster station, where kindly middle-aged ladies were waiting with cups of hot coffee. One of the men mocked their inelegant openwork stockings and was quickly told to shut up: these were obviously wartime make-dos. We boarded again and traveled on to Southampton, where we were marched in formation through dark streets to the Channel dockside.

We then boarded ships that took us on an all-day trip across the water to Le Havre, zigzagging again, but this time to avoid mines. There, after another march to a freight yard, we loaded into World War I-era boxcars called forty-and-eights (*quarante hommes, huite chevaux*), for a rattling, seemingly interminable trip eastward. After several days of moving at two-legged speed (when the boredom and discomfort of sitting or lying on the car's steel floor became too great, we could jump out and walk alongside), we reached the replacement depot ("repple depple") outside Givet, at the tip of the finger France pokes into Belgium. A few weeks earlier, the counter-attacking Germans had tried and failed to cross the Meuse there.

After most of our original Fort McClellan bunch and Queen Elizabeth shipmates hived off to other depots, Murray and I sought out each other's company even more eagerly than before. Some of the GIs at the Givet repple depple were veterans returning to their units after recovering from a wound or an illness. They were easy to spot: their combat fatigues, helmet liners, boots, and packs didn't have the fresh sheen ours had; and they did not have our unknowing and tentative expressions. They seemed preoccupied, their minds elsewhere. They were assigned to the same daily duties—ration breakdown, KP, latrine detail, policing the area (ASSES AND ELBOWS! again)—but they performed these chores with an air of detachment that impressed the rest of us. They knew chicken shit from the real thing.

Murray—always on the lookout for new experiences—latched onto one of these veterans, a smallish, wiry Philadelphian named Albert Brown. Brown had sad eyes, a pencil-thin mustache, and a stoop he must have inherited from generations of sweatshop workers, all making him look as old and wise and familiar as one of our uncles. He always seemed worried and as if he were desperately looking for escape—from us, we began to realize—but also from something else we could not quite identify. But, because Brown was our best hope for finding out what we vaguely but urgently had to know, we tailed him everywhere and badgered him to tell us what IT was really like. He kept putting us off, saying he had nothing to tell us; but finally, his eyes darting about for that escape path and not finding it, as if in deep pain, he forced out between clenched teeth: "KEEP YOUR ASSES LOW!" and hunched off. Murray and I looked at each other with looks on our faces that asked, "Is this the sum of battlefield wisdom?" After that, we left Brown in peace. (As it happened, he was returning to the very infantry company to which I was soon to be assigned.)

Official advice, on the other hand, was all too readily offered. It came in the lectures that all replacements were required to attend every day. We would file into a makeshift auditorium in a huge, drafty tent, three or four hundred in a shift, the eager beavers commandeering the front plank benches, the indifferent ones hanging about at the back. There we listened to lectures with titles such as "World Events," "Why We Fight," "Personal Hygiene in the Field," and "How to Prevent VD"— which seemed to be the Army's idea of a joke, since the only women we ever saw were squat, ruddy, middle-aged French peasants in aprons and blue-checked cotton dresses. They hung around the camp not to pick us up, but rather to snag small jobs, or any food, cigarettes, or candy on offer.

"Personal Hygiene" was one of the more memorable lectures, not least because it was delivered by a round-faced, squeaky-voiced lieutenant with a New York accent. To take a bath in the field, he told us, you should simply detach the metal cup from your canteen, heat the water (it was a little unclear how we were supposed to do this in combat), and pour the hot water into your steel helmet (after you had separated it from its plastic liner). Then, with the small bar of soap you got in your K-rations, you were supposed to carefully lather successive parts of your body and rinse with cupped handfuls of water. It being winter (the coldest in many years, we later learned), the lieutenant did not comment on whether we would have either the opportunity or the fortitude to peel off the layers of t-shirts, boxer shorts, long johns (two pair), pants (two pair), woolen shirts (two), sweaters, combat jackets, mufflers, socks (two pair), woolen under-caps, and gloves that we had been issued at Kilmer and that had been added to by our loving families. But he had clearly given a lot of thought to how each body part should be washed, and he described the technique to be applied to each with almost sensual detail. Then, reminding himself just in time that most of us were barbarians from beyond the civilized pale of the Hudson, his New York accent pitched to a squeaky high C as he chanted, "Remembah, foist yuh face, den yuh cock an' balls! Foist yuh face, den yuh cock an' balls! . . . ."

The next afternoon, convinced that "Personal Hygiene" could not be topped, we settled in for another snoozer. The lecturer for "Care and Maintenance of Equipment" was a raspy-voiced, no-nonsense non-com who, unlike Lieutenant Cock an' Balls, at least seemed to have been there. The information was the usual. We had been through it a million times: how to maintain our rifles, ammo, and webbed cartridge belts; how to use our first-aid kits, bandoliers, water purification tablets, and government issue foot powder; and how to wash our socks (dried by being placed under the layers of our clothes, next to the skin). After this familiar litany of dos and don'ts, Sergeant Raspy-Voice paused, and four hundred men groaned inwardly, thinking "Here we go again . . . ." "Now," he continued,

> Yer combat boots." [Pause] "You all know that Trench Foot is a serious problem in combat." [Pause] "You all know that Trench Foot is caused by lack of circulation in cold, wet feet." [Pause] "You're all familiar with dubbin."[Pause] "You've been taught to keep dubbin' on yer boots at all times." [Pause] Then, with a sigh, he continued, "Now, I want to tell you . . . ["Here it comes," we thought.]"When you're in the field, . . . NEVER! [Pause] NEVER! [Pause] NEVER—USE—DUBBIN—ON—YER—BOOTS! BECAUSE—[Pause]—DUBBIN'—[Pause]—FREEZES—HELL—[Pause]—OUT—OF—YER—FEET!

We were dumbstruck as we took in what he had just said. Then, the huge tent exploded as four hundred combat-bound men roared with delight. IT'S OVER! The days of dubbin', of chicken shit, are over!

5.

SOLDIERS IMPERSONATING SOLDIERS

"Mass paths and other useless roads,
devastated by street battles,
and soldiers impersonating soldiers . . .
still come into my dreams."

Medbh McGuckian, *Filming the Famine*

The weak January light of the Ardennes barely penetrated the gloom of the bunker where I reported for duty. Company E, Second Battalion, Twelfth Regiment, Fourth Infantry Division was holed up along the Siegfried Line. A tall, angular, and fierce-looking first lieutenant with GI steel frame glasses confronted me: "Name? MOS?" I handed him the assignment form with my name, rank, serial number, and military occupation specialty number—my MOS. I think it was 803. To my response, he asked, "What's that number?" "Bugler, sir," I answered. The lieutenant barked a laugh, "Not much for buglers to do around here. You'll be in my Second Platoon, first squad." He had nothing to add, except to say that his name was Patrick J. Tuohy, and the Company was in reserve, waiting to be committed back into battle. I also now had a new MOS: 745—Rifleman.

Second Platoon's quarters were gloomier still. They also had a stench that I would come to recognize after crawling through many more bunkers and trenches recently evacuated by loose-bowelled German soldiers. Mixed with that was the lingering odor of the watery stew that must have caused their digestive trouble and, even in the gelid air, the perpetual reek of GI sweat. In the foreground, a few faces, shadowy in the flickering lantern light, turned toward me; and, along the walls behind them, I could just make out blanketed human shapes stretched out at various levels. It was as if I was seeing a ghost movie, its out-of-focus, underexposed images reflecting my own disorientation. A face told me where to put my backpack, sleeping bag, gas mask, and M-1. Then, from the background, one of the shapes drawled, "Haow long since ya left the States?" I replied, "Two weeks," and trying to take the chill off my welcome, I burbled in my best "Why We Fight" indoctrination mode about bright city lights, busy crowds, and high home-front morale. In response, it was all silence in the bunker. I shut up and crawled into my sleeping bag.

The enlisted man's sleeping bag bore no resemblance to the thick, down-filled, womb-like affair that was one of the prerogatives of being an officer; it was nothing more than a regulation army blanket cut into a mummy shape, with a waterproofed cotton cover and a break-free zipper. It wasn't overly warm and didn't cushion me against the unforgiving steel surface of the bunker shelves, but I was able to sleep in it that first night. The next thing I knew, it was morning, and our assistant squad leader, Sgt. Carroll was rousing us out for duty. Orders had come to move out. We breakfasted hurriedly on our K-Rations, collected our weapons and gear, and formed into squads. The Army Table of Organization stipulated that a squad was to have fifteen men; but, whether by intention or a lack of manpower, few ever did. Seven or eight was a more effective number for sharing messages and deploying quickly. Rifles slung over our shoulders, we shambled off down a country road in a single column. Along the route, our squad leader, Sergeant Keller, dropped back for a word with us, his men. When he came to me, he said in his high tenor Louisiana drawl, "We're movin' up to the lahn to attack a town call' Proom" "Naow," he added kindly, "Don't you be nuhvus. You jes' watch and do what the rest of us do." Then he passed to the next man, giving me no chance to ask questions. It didn't matter: like the foolish son in the Passover Hagadah, I knew not what to ask.

As we moved up toward the town, I pared down my gear to what I could see the other men carrying. I unbuckled and wriggled out of my backpack and dropped it by the side of the road, discarding, along with other comforts, the two sets of woolen long johns my mother had forced on me. I saved one extra pair of dry socks, stuffing them inside my shirt, next to my skin. I tossed away my gas mask, saving its canvas sack for the odd orange or apple, or whatever food I might scrounge up. Unauthorized abandonment of equipment was a violation of Army rules; but Army rules were invented by rear-echelon commandos who did not come up to the line to enforce them. The first combat rule was to make sure there was nothing between you and the ground when you came under fire. You threw yourself down to get as close to Mother Earth as you could. (Brown's grudging advice to Murray and me in the Givet repple depple came back to me: "Keep your asses low!") Cartridge belts, first aid kits, canteens, ammo bandoliers, steel helmets, entrenching tools, hand grenades, and rifles we kept. I carried other baggage too; it was there along with the extra pair of dry socks, but deeper inside. It had more to do with the kind of soldier I wanted to be than all the lectures, the firing practice, and the training films. I couldn't have thrown that away if I tried.

By the time we got to Prüm, some of the other units were already there, and we followed them in, moving from street to street, taking cover in doorways and behind remnants of walls. German and American shells were ripping up the little that was left of the town, already heavily damaged in the seesaw battle just concluded. From the trucks that had carried me up to the line, I had seen some of the worst destruction of earlier battles. St. Vith in Belgium (mistakenly bombed by our own planes) had made the starkest impression: a single wall standing amid the rubble while bull dozers buzzed about like bees on a honeycomb. But in Prüm, I was no longer a war tourist, no longer rubbernecking at damage inflicted by others from the backs of trucks. Prüm was where I came under fire for the first time, although I didn't once fire my rifle as I moved through the town. Crumbled walls and collapsed roofs were not merely details of a war landscape observed from a distance, but markers of success—and cover.

I quickly learned to distinguish between the numbing whistle of the enemy's "incoming mail" and the reassuring blast of our own artillery, to identify an 88-millimeter shell, a mortar round, and the Nebelwerfer rockets we called Screaming Meemies. I also learned to freeze when I heard the long, unholy *brrrrr* of the MG 42, the Germans' terrifying machine gun. During a lull in the combat, a big man with a swooping black mustache and a self-confidant grin appeared—it was Sgt. Kline, our platoon sergeant, one of the men told me. Kline waved us forward, and we scurried from doorway to doorway until we had made our way through town. By then, machine gun fire had died down and incoming shells receded. It was late afternoon. If I felt a little frustrated, even sheepish, at not having fired my weapon, I knew I had done what infantrymen are meant to do: I had taken and held ground.

Later we learned that Sgt. Kline had been stunned by an exploding shell and evacuated. Sgt. Keller had fallen behind and was nowhere to be seen. The word was that, since returning to the line after having been wounded, Keller was likely to do that—often disappearing at the start of a battle, but then showing up again after the shelling stopped. But this time he didn't show up. A big rangy Texan named Fitzgerald, first name S.B., took over for him, while Kline was replaced by Sgt. Wade, a calm Louisianan with a fatherly manner. (He was thirty-eight, but seemed ancient to me.)

By the time we had pushed through Prüm, it was growing dark, and we were ordered to take up positions in an abandoned German trench beyond the far side of town. The Heinies (never called "Germans" or "Jerries" or "Krauts" in our outfit) were nowhere to be seen, but when night fell, their artillery launched a barrage, much heavier now. Some of the shells exploded so close to our trench, we could hear the shrapnel zinging over our huddled bodies like mosquitoes searching for blood. There was nowhere to hide and nothing to do but cringe and wait for the explosion and flash, then hunker down again until the next. All night the shelling continued, all night the expectation of instant obliteration or—worse—ripped up flesh. Those 88s, with their abrupt whistle turning into a drawn-out scream, burned a permanent scar in my nervous system. (Sixty-five years later, the sound of incoming shells in a war film jolts me like an electric current until my wife takes my hand.) As if the shelling was not scary enough, one of my squad mates, Hershel Repton, kept up a steady wail of doom: hunched over, arms around knees, slightly rocking, the whites of his eyes shining in the moonlight against the dark background of his unshaven cheeks, he cried over and over in his country drawl: "Oh, my, oh my, we gonna get it tonight; oh my, oh my, tonight shoh!" I would hear that dirge again many times, and it always made me feel murderous, especially when we had to move out and Hershel stayed, cowering on the ground. We cursed him and threatened to hit him with a rifle butt to make him get up. Poor Hershel! He was too old and too attached to his Tennessee farm, his wife, and his kids to be up there sweating Heinie shells.

The morning light brought relief. The guns were distant thunder now, too far away to worry about, and the chatter of small arms had stopped. We climbed out of the trench, formed into a single column, and set off, careful to keep a good interval between us in case the firing started up again. Chasing a retreating enemy was exhilarating and helped shake off the funk of the trench. As we fanned out over a grassy field, advancing on a wooded patch about a mile ahead, I suddenly saw myself—steel helmeted, slightly crouching, rifle at the ready—the image of a soldier impersonating a soldier. (Look at me, Pa! Look at me, girls! Look at me, Jew haters!) Suddenly I spotted some figures, dark against a distant hillside. Heinies! I whipped up my rifle and squeezed off a round. There was a scream of pain—not from the Germans, since they were beyond our range—but from Sgt. Boudreaux, leader of the third platoon. I had fired off my maiden shot inches from his ear!

That night it snowed, and the snow continued to fall and cover the frozen ground for the next few weeks of what turned out to be the coldest winter in Europe in twenty years. Most nights, we dug slit trenches to sleep in and covered them with shelter halfs, the half of a pup tent each of us was supposed to carry. They were actually kept somewhere in the rear and, together with blankets, were dropped off for us—when possible—by jeeps that darted up to the line and hurried back to greater safety. Boots were supposed to stay on in case we were surprised during the night, but I couldn't sleep with my sore feet encased in them; so I usually took them off, grabbing for them first thing in the morning.

The days repeated themselves. Waking at first light and consuming our breakfast K-rations (the tightly packed, loathsome pork & egg yolk combo in a can and canteen cups of powdered coffee—if we were were able to make a fire), we would then jump off to begin our chase of the enemy. One man was lead scout, or point man, followed by the second scout, with the rest of the squad fanning out behind him, the terrain determining the distance and spacing separating them. We spread out over the rightly named Schnee Eifel (Snow Hills), bunching up—sometimes almost touching—when we had to pass through the many wooded areas where visibility and security were more problematic. Somewhere toward the rear were our officers, the good ones, like Lt. Tuohy, constantly moving back and forth among us. The standard practice was to rotate our tactical assignments, each member of a squad taking his turn as first scout, or point man, one day, second scout the next, and so on. After a few days, I made a decision: I would take the first scout position permanently. I don't know if I was trying to prove something to myself or was just reluctant to hitch my fate to the likes of Repton. Maybe some of both, but with no one objecting, I was the squad's point man from that day forward—well, at least until my feet failed me some months later.

We pushed across the easternmost reaches of the Schnee Eifel, wading freezing streams at night, taking prisoners, occasionally meeting half-hearted resistance, and trying not to think about what we would run into when we got to the Rhine. Sometimes as we slogged through a village just emptied of retreating Heinies, I amused myself by singing my high school version of "Lili Marlene" or "Ich hatte einen Kameradin," startling some local woman watching us passing her gate. Once I spied a German soldier standing alone and unarmed in a field ahead of us. He looked bewildered and dejected. I approached, pointing my rifle at him and asked my stock prisoner question: "Wo sind di anderen?" (Where are the others?). He barely acknowledged my presence, whining that he had not had anything to eat for "sechs Stunden" (six hours). I relayed this information to Lt. Tuohy, who snorted "tough shit, neither have we!" I ordered him to put his hands on his head and sent him scuttling back to our rear lines where, I thought, he would probably be fed something better than the K-rations that we had to look forward to for our evening meal. But just ahead were two surprises. First, in a quiet patch of woods, the company mess truck was waiting for us; with its soup pots steaming, and its portable oven laden with roasting chickens. This moveable feast was presided over by a three-stripe sergeant of familiar Sephardic face and imposing figure—Victor Aresty, an older brother of my friend Jerry! (He was the one we always called "the Turk.")

After expressions of mutual surprise and delight, Vic told me that when the Battle of the Bulge began a little more than a month earlier, he had been mess sergeant of Easy Company. The 12th Regiment, having been badly mauled in the Huertgen Forest, had been assigned to a quiet sector in Luxembourg, and Easy Company was billeted in an abandoned hat factory in the town of Echternach. When the Germans attacked, Easy Company was surrounded and cut off. The men fought hard for several days, taking lots of casualties, but with no way out they finally surrendered. Loaded on German trucks, a few of them, including Vic, jumped off and ran into a wooded area where they hid until they could make their way back to the American lines. The Easy Company that Vic had known no longer existed; it had been reconstituted with strangers, transfers from other outfits, and replacements like myself. (Even Lt. Touhy was a newcomer, having gone through the battles of the Huertgen and the Bulge in another unit.) When we met, Vic was saying his goodbyes. As a "high point man" (he had been in combat since D-Day) and an escaped prisoner (a special category), he was being flown home for early discharge.

The effect on me of this encounter was complicated. Seeing someone from home, someone who was almost family, was hugely reassuring; but I had the sense that it was also a ceremony of maturation, a kind of battlefield *bar mitzvah*. I was no longer one of the kids under big brother Vic's feet, but an equal, a member of the same fraternity of combat veterans. It had another, less happy consequence. When Vic returned to Rochester a week or so later, he went to see my parents and assured them that I was safe and well. But—I suppose to make them proud—he went on to tell them of my single-handed capture of the hungry German soldier. This confirmed what they already feared: my rosy accounts in letters home to them were false; I was not lounging in rear echelon safety and comfort, but risking life and limb. Now my mother had something very real to worry about!

That March, we were quite suddenly pulled out of the line and told we were going into reserve. As we later learned, the Fourth Division was being transferred from Patton's Third Army to Alexander Patch's Seventh. Elements of the First Infantry Division were coming in to relieve us. The first I knew of this, a guy with a Big Red One shoulder patch was lowering himself into my foxhole. Trucks appeared, each with a machine gun sticking out of its cabin roof, and we rode back off the line to a quiet country area in France, somewhere between Metz and Nancy. We spent the better part of a blissful week there, eating, playing softball on a diamond we scratched out in a field, and sleeping through nights uninterrupted by shellfire.

Our idyll ended just as abruptly as it had begun. Trucks re-appeared, and we were carried back southeast toward the front, which had meanwhile advanced toward the Rhine. We were tense, unhappy that our vacation had been cut short, and fearful of going back into combat. Some of the men distracted themselves by swapping insults with men from other squads, lobbing verbal abuse back and forth between the trucks like hand grenades. Smitty, a man from my platoon, worked off his feelings by cursing the African American truck drivers who were taking us to the front, calling them "black bastards." Others joined in. When he himself took a verbal shot from someone in my squad, Smitty fired back: "Wail, ahm glad to say that, in mah squad, we ain't got no "Christ-killers!" Although he didn't look in my direction, he could only have meant me. I said nothing, too preoccupied with thoughts of the coming firefight to get into a pissing match with this redneck bigot. Besides, I sensed that making an issue of my Jewishness among these men would only emphasize my isolation. The men of my platoon were not, by and large, the comrades I would have chosen, but they were the comrades I had.

At Worms, a pontoon bridge had been thrown across the big river. Our trucks bumped down over its track and up the far bank. A few miles on, they dumped us out in open country. We reassembled and resumed our advance on foot, now moving southeastward into Bavaria. It didn't take very long before we learned the difference between chasing retreating Heinies to the Rhine and forcing our way, step by step, into the German heartland. We were crossing an open field, heading toward a stand of woods a few hundred yards ahead of us, when those woods erupted with machine gun fire. Everyone dropped to the ground. From somewhere we heard an order: "Get into the woods!" Reluctantly, each of us raised himself crook-backed and ran forward, bent almost double, and then dropped to the ground, repeating this jack rabbit maneuver several times until we could throw ourselves into the cover of the woods, and sprawl behind a tree or wriggle into an old wagon track. By that time, the firing had stopped, and we cautiously took stock. Pearson, a chubby BAR man (what we called the guys toting Browning Automatic Rifles) in my squad, had been grazed in the head and was very shaken, but our middle-aged medico, Arthur White, calmly applied some sulfa powder and a bandage and sent him walking back to the rear to find an aid station. One man in another squad hadn't made it—shot through the head during our first approach.

Soon the winter light began to fade, and we were told to bed down for the night at the perimeter of the trees. A jeep brought up our bedrolls. I found a V-mail form in my jacket pocket and sat down to write my parents: "Dear Folks, Everything is fine here. I've heard from Rose and Edie, and some of my friends. It looks as though the war will be over soon, and I'll be home before you know it. Hope you are both well. Love, Don." I tucked it back into my pocket for future mailing, unaware that Victor's visit had already blown my cover.

At sunrise we awoke, ate our breakfasts, got our gear together, and formed up to jump off. Not that we went very far or fast. From their concealed position about a hundred yards ahead, the Germans fired sporadically, and we inched forward, hugging the ground, close together to keep contact. We paused at an opening where there were some wagon tracks scarcely qualifying as a road, and when the guns went silent, I jumped up to dash across. I stumbled—a tree root maybe— and sprawled across the clearing, an easy target. I was sure I was a goner. But I found myself intact, pulled myself together, and crawled back to our side of the road, where there was a bit of cover. By then, my squad mate "Heavy" Carter had caught up with me. Grinning at my clumsiness, he started to cross the track, looking back and waving as if to say, "It's ok, come on." There was a burst of machine gun fire and Carter fell, gasping and sobbing. The rest of us emptied our weapons in the direction of the firing, and the German machine guns fell silent again. We cowered at the edge of the road, trying to decide what to do. Lieutenant Ragsdale, our new platoon leader (in the wake of Tuohy's promotion to company commander) caught up with us, took in the situation, and motioned to me to go out to Carter, repeating those classic words I've never been able to understand either in combat or in Western movies: "Go ahead, I'll cover you." Warily, I snaked out to Carter and, with the German guns now silent, raised myself to my hands and knees and only half succeeded in turning him over.

The burst had hit him in the mid-section, and I could see some blood, but not the wound. He had been breathing—barely—but now his body seemed to let go, and he went completely still. Even in my inexperience, I knew he was dead. My first thought: "Go through his pack to see if there's anything I can use—food? candy? dry socks?" My second thought: "Shame! What's happened to me?" I let go of Carter's pack and crawled back to the others. Dreese had brought up the light machine gun, and guys from the weapons platoon set up their mortar. We riddled the woods in front of us. At the same time, we heard firing from both our section and another section, and Lt. Ragsdale went off to see what was going on. We held that position for the rest of the day, waiting for the Lieutenant to return, braced for more German machine gun fire, feeling an eerie isolation from the rest of the company, but uncertain what to do.

When night came, we tried to sleep, this time without our bedrolls because we were beyond the reach of the company jeep. As we were going through our usual breakfast routine the next morning, Cochrane, our company runner, came as though out of nowhere, shouting. "Lt. Ragsdale is dead! Don't take any prisoners!" It seemed a strange admonition since we still hadn't seen a Heinie since we entered the woods, and it increased our confusion, or mine anyway. Then Lt. Tuohy appeared; with Ragsdale gone, he took over his old platoon and pumped some life into us, ordering everyone to his feet. Sounds from other parts of the woods told us that the other platoons were doing likewise and, as we rallied in body and spirit, the cry went out: FORWARD! MARCHING FIRE! I had never heard that command before; maybe none of us had (although supposedly a favorite of our commanding general, Patton) but instinctively, we knew what to do: firing our rifles from the hip, we advanced toward the still invisible enemy, marching in rank like some company of Redcoats crossing Boston Common.

The heavy barrage of fire, the smoke, the screaming of men and shells, and the advancing line seem to have terrified the Germans. From the thick forest ahead of us, makeshift white banners appeared. The men who had killed Carter, Ragsdale, and the other GI (so new to the company that I had not had time to learn his name), the men who for the past two and a half days had been trying to kill the rest of us, now went into their dance of surrender. Springing up, throwing their weapons down, dashing their helmets to the ground, clasping their hands on the top of their heads, muttering, "Kamerad!"—with every movement, declaring submission. Their smug confidence that, by these rituals, they had bowed themselves out of the war filled me with rage; and as they passed me, shuffling toward the rear and to safety, I kicked a couple of them in the ass. They seemed to expect it.

6.

FORWARD SLOPE

"Of course, as a survivor of an infantry company, I was marked by death for life when I was
nineteen."

Samuel Menashe, *New and Selected Poems*

We were like an army of one-legged men, limping in a
deep-plowed turnip field, each with one foot on the
ridge of the furrow, the other in the trough. The February
earth was surprisingly soft. No enemy in sight. Late in the afternoon, we came up a broad rise to a village where we were
sure we would get the order to bed down for the night—maybe
in a hayloft or even on a warm kitchen floor. Not bad; we'd
had worse days.

Lt. Tuohy and Sgt. Wade brought bad news from the
Company command post: we were not staying there; our

assigned objective was a village about a mile further on. Sgt. Wade said the lieutenant had protested the order, arguing that the light was fading, that we had had a long day stumping through the turnip fields, that it would be much easier to take the village in the morning, and that, anyhow, the Heinies seemed to have checked out and were nowhere to be seen. But the CO had told him that Division was just passing down orders from Third Army Headquarters: that next village was part of General Patton's objective for the day, and we had to take it before nightfall. Besides, Division said, turning our officers' argument back on them, no enemy soldiers had been seen or heard from in that village. The way they saw it, there'd be nothing to it. We would simply walk in.

So we picked up our rifles and moved out, grumbling about Army timetables and cursing General Patton—more disappointed and tired than worried. As first scout of the lead squad, I was out in front but not by much; we were deployed wide not deep, with the three rifle platoons almost abreast. The men in weapons platoon followed close behind, one man lugging the mortar barrel, another the plate, a third carrying the heavy, water-cooled 30-caliber machine gun, and the others loaded down with tripods and boxes of ammo. After advancing a few hundred yards, we found ourselves moving upward on rising ground, enough of an angle to remove our objective, the village, from our line of sight. Once we had climbed the hill, the ground dropped off sharply in front of us. The village came in full sight again, about a half mile ahead and well below. We were spread out on the forward slope of the hill, looking down at the village—although in the fading light, we could barely make out its houses and barns.

Suddenly, those houses and barns erupted with a fury. Machine gun fire! We hit the ground, straining frantically to press our heads and arms and legs down into the earth. The Heinies had been sitting down there in that village, waiting for us to come over the brow of the hill. Now they had us on the forward slope, totally exposed and with no place to hide. They were firing continuous bursts, the way German machine gunners always did—*brrrrrrrrrrrrrrr*. The long buzz of the MG 42s always came at you like a string of hornets, and we always wondered how they managed to keep it up without burning out their barrels.

Just hours earlier, as we had walked toward the village, we had cursed the soft soil of the fields for sucking on our boots. Now, I cursed the hard ground of the hillside for refusing to receive us, for not shielding us from the machine guns firing their 2200 (or however many) rounds per minute. With my chin pushing into the ground I stretched my eyeballs almost out of their sockets to look around without raising my head. I could just discern bodies sprawled out on each side. A few men who had run forward instead of back before flinging themselves down stretched out in front of me. A hundred, maybe one-hundred-and-fifty men—practically the whole company—were pinned down on that hillside, unable to advance or retreat. Everywhere, German machine gun bullets were biting into the ground—I could hear them cracking in my ears and saw them out of the corners of my eyes, throwing up little sprays of dirt. I knew we were like ducks in a shooting gallery, but I could not tell how many men were being hit. DO NOT GET CAUGHT ON THE FORWARD SLOPE OF A HILL

IN PLAIN SIGHT OF THE ENEMY! How many times had I heard that in my thirteen weeks of basic training?

Some of the men around me began calling to each other, but it was hard to hear what they were saying above the rattle of the machine guns. Then I heard, "Ah'm goin' back!" I knew that voice—Repton, the Tennessee farmer in my squad. I had spent my first night in combat cowering in a trench with him after we had passed through Prüm, both of us terrified by the screams of the incoming shells. All night long, I had been forced to watch him roll his eyes till the whites showed in the moonlight, and to listen to him moan, "We gonna get it, sho'!" That dismal forecast was Repton's theme song, as I had come to learn. He replayed it every time we were under fire, whether from machine guns, mortar shells, or small arms. Sometimes his fear so immobilized him that we had to threaten to kick or shoot him to make him get up and move out with the squad, which he eventually did. This time he has flipped, I thought. Go back? He was going to get to his feet under that blanket of fire and run back over the crest of the hill? He would be cut down before he raised himself to his knees. "You're crazy," I think I screamed. I saw a blur of a body go past my restricted line of sight. Then I heard someone else whose voice I recognized—L.Z. Morris—saying he was going too. I yelled at him too, but he went. Then another, and another—each man was up and gone. With no non-com or officer within sight or hearing, everyone had to make the decision for himself.

I do not remember how I made mine. I did not know what had happened to Repton or Morris, or the others. I was terrified to go and terrified to stay. Peering out of the corners of my eyes without raising my head, I could see feet move and hear shouts, and I could feel that the area around me was emptying of men. I suppose they created a momentum, and it eventually caught me up—so I went too. Maybe the greater fear won: doing something seemed better than doing nothing. Still, getting up off that piece of ground was the hardest thing I had ever had to do. It seemed there was no way not to get hit. With the air buzzing with MG 42 hornets, I pulled myself to my feet and ran up the slope, back, back—throwing myself the last few yards like a football player flying over the goal line—over the brow of the hill and down to safety.

Now I could see men coming my way, hunched down, catching their breath behind the protective mass of the hill, then getting up to run back to the village we had left so grudgingly all that time ago. Repton, Morris, Carroll, Plunkett, Wade— most of the rest of Second Platoon were already there—and we could see the men of the other platoons milling around, everyone panting and excited and unbelieving, hugging each other. Safe! Safe!

Squad leaders called out the names of their men and looked around to eyeball them. As each name found its living owner, the incredible began to seem believable: we were ALL there; we had all stood up in that storm of fire and run back—twenty, fifty, a hundred yards without a single man of us getting hit! Not quite, though: one man did not answer when his name was called. John Little, Second Platoon, a pink-faced, good-natured farm boy from Tennessee. Alive or dead, Little was still out there on the forward slope of the hill. That dampened the party a bit, but, hell, we were alive.

While Frenchy, Garcia, and the other mess personnel who had remained behind in the village set up their portable stoves for hot chow, platoon leaders huddled with the CO, who was on the radio to Division. Lt Tuohy came back with the word: Army had cancelled the designated objective for that day; we would spend the night where we were. Already our artillery was shelling that nest of German machine guns. Stomachs filled, nerves settling down, we gathered the bedrolls that had been brought up in the Company jeep and spread them on the floors of the houses we had commandeered. Everyone except the man on guard went to sleep.

In the middle of the night, voices woke me: the guard had challenged someone, and then waved him on into our house. The door closed, and a candle was lit. John Little stood there, blinking. Around him, the men of Second Platoon were starting up as they recognized him. Then everyone began shouting at him at once—greetings and questions and straight-faced jokes. Stretched out on that hillside, caught under that sheet of fire, the logic of John's cold terror had taken him to a different conclusion: for John, getting up was worse than staying, so he stayed. All the time the rest of us were making our run for it— really just a moment or two—he was waiting for the bullet that had his number on it, too scared to take the crazy chance of getting up. By the time the German machine guns had stopped firing, it was growing dark, and we had evaporated. Then (finally) our own artillery began bombarding the town, the first shells screaming in just in front of him as the guns bracketed their target. Now there was really no way he could go.

Our guns went still sometime during the night, and Little's fear began to thaw. He got to his feet and, in the dark, stumbled back up, then over and down the hill to the village. Now, encircled by the men of his platoon, finally safe, he sank to the floor, trembling, and sobbed. For a long, painful, silent moment, we stood and watched, each of us absorbed in his own thoughts. Then, we turned back to our sleeping bags. In the morning, we ate our breakfast K-rations, talking less than usual; and, once more, we moved out toward our objective, the village. We were wary, but our artillery barrage had done its work; the Heinie machine gunners and their comrades had disappeared during the night. We simply walked in.

7.

SNIPERS

We had walked all morning following a railroad track, single file in the draw alongside the raised track bed. It was easy going, and we kept up a good pace with no resistance. Our next objective was a small town with a name I have forgotten. The monotony of our progress was interrupted when a shell screamed in. We hit the ground. No damage. Somebody said it was from a Kraut 20 mm. flak gun—pretty light stuff—but after that we crawled.

It was sheer misery. Stones had tumbled down from the track bed into the draw, along with bits of broken glass, cans, pieces of wire, and all the other garbage you find along railroad tracks everywhere, even in Germany. As we dragged ourselves and our weapons along, sweating in the weak March sun, glass and wire dug into our palms and knees, pieces of tin scraped flesh and caught on the bulging pockets of our fatigues and combat jackets; and the upturned stones engaged with canteens, ammo bandoliers, cartridge belts, hand grenades, and gas mask bags stuffed with whatever. We cursed and raged, our helmets slipping over our eyes. Every few minutes some poor bastard, unable to take it any longer, jumped up and ran more or less upright—until a shell whistled in and he would drop down again to crawl in the ditch with the rest of us.

That ditch seemed endless, although we actually reached the first houses of the town in a couple of hours. Getting into a town was always exhilarating, especially if getting there had been tough. You could see a town and read its name. It was a tangible goal; reaching it was progress to somewhere, proof that crawling in the ditch and taking enemy fire had paid off—as long as you were not hit. A town meant rest, cover, maybe finding something to eat other than cold K-Rations. If it was late enough in the day for an overnight stop, we might be lucky enough to find a bed or a warm kitchen floor, or at least a hayloft instead of a waterlogged slit trench to sleep in.

After waiting to make sure the Heinie flak gun was no longer zeroed in on us, we stormed into the streets like hot air rushing from a balloon, propelled by the frustration and rage of the ditch and the promise of the town. A shot broke our momentum. Another shot. Snipers! The Heinies had held their fire, taken concealed positions, and waited for us to show ourselves in the streets. Now they were trying to pick us off, slow us down. They could not have had much hope of driving us back, but they were going to make every step miserable for us; they wanted to make sure we would take casualties. We found cover in doorways, stairwells, anywhere; but we knew we were going to have to find the snipers and flush them out.

We paired off and started. I was with Plunkett, one of our squad's BAR men. Standard operating procedure was for one man to provide cover, while the other kicked the door open and exploded into a room yelling and cursing, and making as much commotion as possible. The idea was to startle and terrify anyone inside, so they would have no time to defend themselves—or, more to the point, no time to see that we were as vulnerable and scared as they were. Every room Plunkett and I charged into was empty. Coming out of a house, I saw Lt. Tuohy standing by a doorway trying to tell a half-dozen bewildered and frightened townspeople to take shelter in the church; but the lieutenant did not know any German, and they did not know any English. He called me over to translate with my mix of high school German and family Yiddish. "Gehen sie in" . . . "Gehen sie nach" . . . Christ, I could not for the life of me remember the word for church!—not in my family's lexicon. I did not know what to do except repeat myself over and over, "Gehen sie, gehen sie"—until Tuohy put his hands together as if he were praying, and they got the idea, saying "Kirche, Kirche!" Tuohy picked it up and yelled, "Keersha! Keersha!" alternating between putting his hands together and pointing toward the church spire. Off they went, crouching and zigzagging toward the church, as terrified of the snipers as we were.

Meanwhile, Plunkett had gone on his way alone up the street, so I went back to searching houses on my own—unhappily, since that BAR he carried had a lot more fire power and made a lot more noise than my M-1. I came to the end of the street, feeling a little more confident because I had not run into any enemy soldiers yet. I had a set procedure: I would get into the entry way as fast and quietly as I could, then let out a roar and kick open the door of the first room, dash in yelling "Raus Hände Hoch! RAUS! RAUS!" When I had repeated the routine for every room, I would go on to the next house.

I turned into the next street, dashed into the first house, bellowed into one room, then another. I stopped. There, in the second room, in a narrow bed, lay a man. A blanket covered him to his chin. He was neither too old nor too young to be a soldier, and he was not asleep. He could not have been as startled by me as I was by him, since he had to have heard me when I stormed into the first room. I assumed that he had been sniping at us from the house, and, not knowing what else to do when he heard me coming in, that he had gotten into bed and covered up. Heinie sonofabitch probably had his rifle under that blanket too.

"RAUS, RAUS VOM BETT!" I yelled. He did not stir. I screamed the words again and waved the muzzle of my M-1 at him. He muttered something, tight-mouthed, and moved his head in refusal. Only then did I look into his face—damp and waxen skin stretched tight across his cheeks and an expression that combined listlessness and sullen defiance, but nothing I could see as fear. Instead, it was a kind of indifference that made me feel both furious and powerless; here I was pointing a loaded rifle at the sneaky bastard son-of-a-bitch, and I couldn't get him to move! Did he have a firearm or a grenade under the blanket? I raged and screamed at him, but he kept shaking his head slowly and muttering something that sounded like "nay," and looking off to the side. Finally, I grabbed a corner of the blanket and—while he made a feeble effort to hold it down— yanked it away and dropped it on the floor. I froze.

A small, wasted creature, his head too big for his body, he lay there curled up in a fetal position. His shrunken arms and legs could not have supported him; they must have always been like that. He was naked except for dingy underpants, his yellow skin shadowed with a greenish tinge, as though it had never seen daylight. He smelled of sweat, stale air, filthy bed-clothes, and despair.

I stared. I mumbled apologetic and absurdly formal phrases from my high school German book: "Es tut mir Leid! Entschuldigen Sie mich!" But he was out of reach, and these polite courtesies sounded ridiculous even as I mouthed them. He muttered again, impatiently, angrily, something I could not quite catch, pushed into the gray rumpled sheet as if he were trying to hide from me—or to dismiss me as irrelevant. I reached down for the blanket and began to cover him. As I did, he turned his head. Our eyes met—and held. He began to whimper. As I frantically repeated my useless apologies, a few tears trickled down his contorted face. I let go of the blanket. I ran out of the house.

In the street, I rejoined the men of my platoon. They had flushed out all the snipers and were herding them together. Dropping their weapons, the prisoners threw off their helmets and locked their hands on their heads. We left them to find their way to the rear; there was no need to put a guard over them; they were happy to be out of the fray. A convent cellar yielded bottles of Schnapps, Kirchwasser, and wine. The town was ours. The celebration began.

8.

ATROCITY

Wet and shivering, our platoon came out of the rain-sogged woods into a clearing. Through the late afternoon gloom, we saw a huddle of buildings about three hundred yards east of us. We headed toward them, walking cautiously, spread well apart. Suddenly, shells began screaming in— German 88s, followed by the machine guns, the long steady *brrrrr* of the MG-42s. The ground was too flat and open to provide any cover, so my squad ran toward the dark buildings and dashed into the first house we came to. We threw ourselves down on the kitchen floor, panting and thankful for its warmth and protection. Now the 88s seemed to be zeroing in on us. We appeared to be in a little village. Machine gun bursts were coming from somewhere outside the perimeter of the houses; but, in the fading light, we couldn't tell from where, so we couldn't return their fire.

When we started to take stock of our situation, it seemed that we were the only squad of the platoon that had made it into the houses. We guessed that the others were still in the woods with the rest of Easy Company, or that they had taken cover at the edge of the clearing when they saw that we had come under fire. We could not tell whether the machine gun fire and shelling were the parting shots of the Germans we had been chasing all day or the beginnings of a counter-attack. There was no sign of any civilians; they had probably evacuated the village when they saw that it was right in the line of fire from both sides. We seven were eerily alone, surrounded, we feared, by an enemy we could not see.

Dreese, Peterson, and I covered the side of the house that faced east. Between us and a cluster of houses about 200 yards further on, there was a grassy open space—a sort of village common—and we strained our eyes to spot anyone who might try to cross it. The others took up positions at windows and doors that gave them a view back to the west, the way we had come. We were hoping to see the rest of the company coming to join us, but we were worried that Heinies counter-attacking from the East would arrive first.

The alarm came on my side. Dreese, Rendell, and I almost simultaneously made out a shape moving toward us across the grassy opening, then another, then a third. We began firing. Rendell got off short bursts of his BAR, while I squeezed off some rounds with my M-1. Dreese had set his tripod on the floor and opened up with the 30-caliber light machine gun through an open window. After a moment Rendell stopped firing and began to shout. In a split second, as the shapes came into view, I could see why: they weren't German soldiers but civilian villagers, a man and two women. I shouted too, but Dreese kept firing his machine gun. We yelled louder: OK! Civilians! Stop! Dreese still didn't seem to hear. We kept screaming at him, but he seemed fused to the gun, firing short steady bursts, staring out, his face frozen in dead concentration. One of the women dropped, Dreese still firing; then the man went down, then the other woman. Only then did he stop. He sat on the floor, staring, not moving, next to his weapon, while Rendell and I, joined by Whitey, our medic, ran out to the grassy opening.

The two women, heavy-set middle-aged peasant types, head-scarved, lay motionless in the grass. The man, grey-haired, also chunky, in a dark corduroy jacket, brimmed hat on the ground, was kneeling, apparently unhurt, by the side of one of the women, holding her hand—"meine Frau," he said dully. Whitey checked her over; she was dead. The woman next to her was alive, but apparently in shock; her leg shattered. "Die Schwester," the man explained, whether his or his wife's he didn't say. Whitey applied sulfa powder, bandaged the leg, and gave her a shot of morphine while I tried to express our regrets. "Es tut uns leid," I told him in my feeble German, trying to explain that, in the murky light, we had thought they were German soldiers and realized our mistake too late. He was clearly distraught, but passive, and deferential, like most of the German villagers we had met, and said little more. A couple of the other guys came out to help and to move the sister out of the clearing. The wife's dead body was left there.

Back in the house, Dreese was still sitting on the floor at his machine gun, just as we had left him, but he began to speak, dully, a few words, to no one in particular. He hadn't been able to see that they were civilians, he said, and couldn't understand why we were shouting. He had stopped firing as soon as he realized his mistake. His voice was quiet, even matter-of-fact, his expression deadpan, with no sign of anguish. He stood up, took a K-ration box out of his jacket, sat down on the floor again, opened it and began chewing the biscuits, slowly, evenly. I was amazed at his calm. I didn't believe him. He must have been able to make out the figures of the civilians at the same time that we did; he must have heard us screaming at him! He had only stopped after they were all down. I sensed that the others were skeptical too, but no one voiced it. We wolfed down some cold pressed meat from our supper K-rations and smoked, taking care to shield the flare of the matches and the glow of the cigarettes from the windows as we continued peering out.

Soon the enemy machine gun firing ceased, and then the artillery became increasingly sporadic, ultimately stopping altogether during the night. Our little cluster of houses had not been stormed, and we took turns getting some sleep. In the morning the rest of the Company arrived, a platoon at a time, without incident, and took up positions in the other houses. We knew then that the German barrage had been a rear guard action covering the retreat. There were no German forces anywhere near the village. The rain had stopped, and we felt secure enough to make fires and heat up our breakfast ration: pork minced with egg yolks in a can, crackers, powdered lemonade, and instant coffee. Once we had filled our bellies, we moved out to chase the Germans.

Was Dreese quieter than usual? It was hard to tell; he had never been much of a talker. No one said anything about what had happened, not to Dreese, not to each other, certainly not to our non-coms or officers. The next time promotions were handed out, Dreese made sergeant.

Whenever I looked at Dreese after that, I could not help but see the image of him hunched over his chattering gun, his eyes with that dead expression fixed on the grassy opening out ahead of us. I went over it in my mind a hundred times and decided that, when he saw those figures coming at us in the gloom, something in him must have given way. At that point, possessed by fear and hatred, it made no difference that they were civilians; anyone in his sights would have paid the price. An "uncontrollable rage," I suppose a psychologist might now call it. But was it a deliberate killing? Was it a crime? Then it came to me: if Dreese was guilty of a crime, so were all of us—all of us who had been there and seen it, and now kept quiet. We were not guilty of the killing ("murder" was a word I never applied to it), but we shared his guilt nevertheless; because we had let it pass, made no accusation, voiced not a word of reproach. We had not even framed the question. As much as this troubled my 19-year old conscience, I was not about to become Dreese's accuser; the consequences were unthinkable— for him, for the squad, for me—and I pushed the thought as far away from me as I could.

"Hell," I told myself, "it's the goddamned war."

Made in the USA
Monee, IL
30 March 2021